AROUND THE WORLD
OCEANIA &
SOUTH AMERICA

A TRAVEL MEMOIR

Daily chronicles of
life on the road backpacking

By Christopher D. Morgan

*To my darling wife, Sandy.
Thank you for putting up with me
for over 400 days on the road.*

Around the world: OCEANIA & SOUTH AMERICA
Daily chronicles of life on the road backpacking

Copyright © 2024 Christopher & Sandy Morgan
All rights reserved.

No part of this text may be reproduced, transmitted, downloaded, decompiled, reverse engineered or stored in or introduced into any information storage and retrieval system, in any form or by any means, whether electronic or mechanical, now known or hereafter invented, without the express permission of the author except for use of brief quotations in book reviews.

This travel memoir has been written using British English spelling and conventions.

All photographs copyright © Christopher & Sandy Morgan

Formatted & edited by Christopher Morgan

First edition

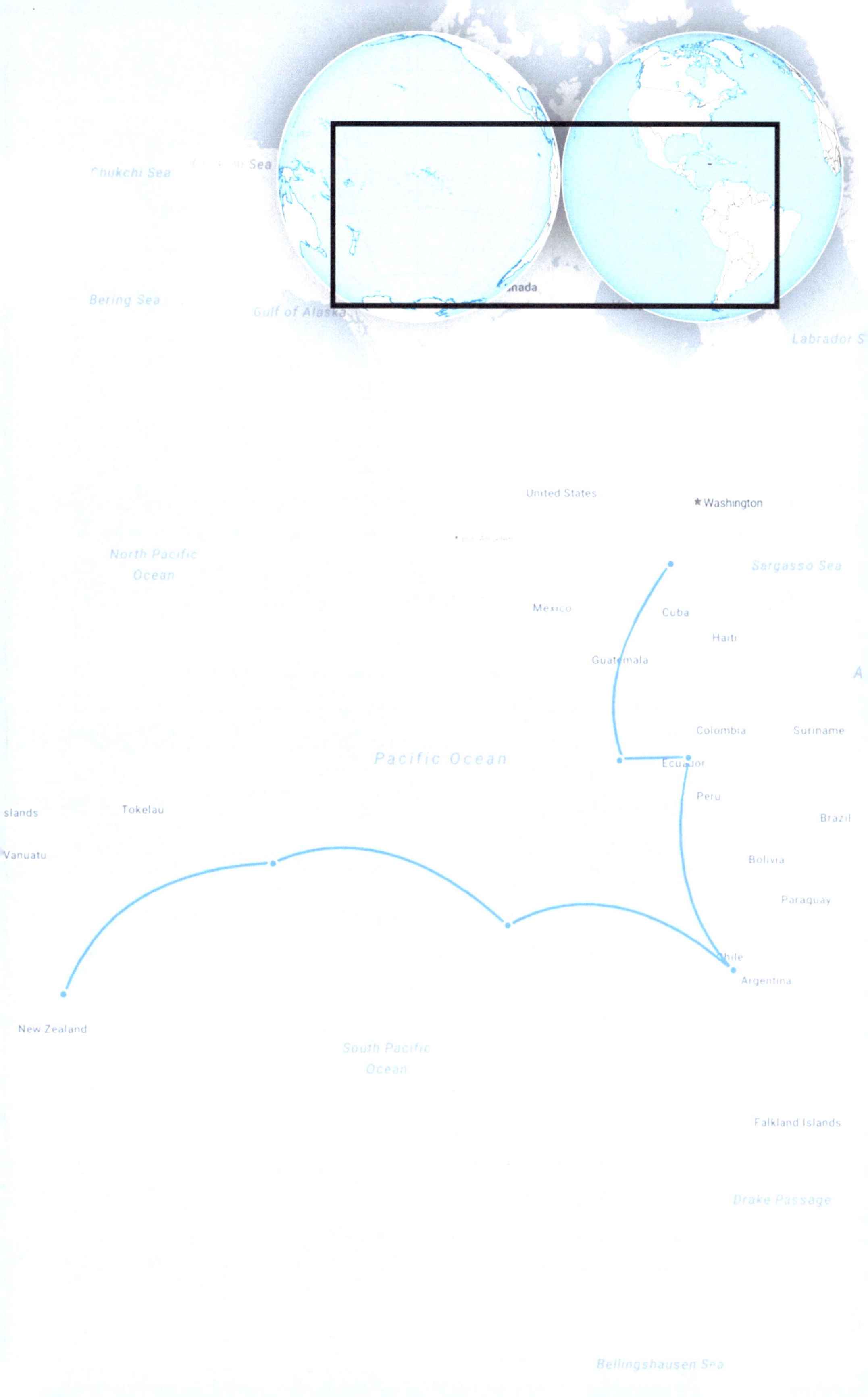
Chukchi Sea
Bering Sea
Gulf of Alaska
United States
Washington
North Pacific Ocean
Sargasso Sea
Mexico
Cuba
Haiti
Guatemala
Colombia
Suriname
Pacific Ocean
Ecuador
Peru
Tokelau
Vanuatu
Brazil
Bolivia
Paraguay
Chile
Argentina
New Zealand
South Pacific Ocean
Falkland Islands
Drake Passage
Bellingshausen Sea

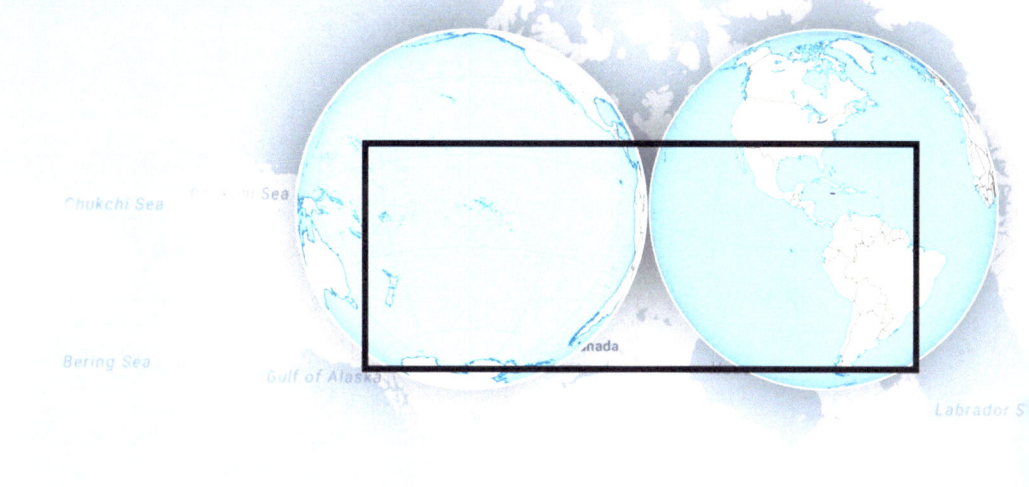

CONTENTS

INTRODUCTION 1
    Travel Memoirs 1
    The decision to go travelling 2
    Where to travel to 6
    What to take with us 7
    Documenting the journey 9

TAHITI 11
    Day 387: Wednesday, 30th March, 2005, Papeete 11
    Day 388: Thursday, 31st March, 2005, Papeete 16

EASTER ISLAND 23
    Day 389: Saturday, 2nd April, 2005, Hanga Roa 23
    Day 390: Sunday, 3rd April, 2005, Hanga Roa 32
    Day 391: Monday, 4th April, 2005, Hanga Roa 40
    Day 392: Tuesday, 5th April, 2005, Hanga Roa 47

CHILE 55
    Day 393: Wednesday, 6th April, 2005, Santiago 55
    Day 394: Thursday, 7th April, 2005, Santiago 62

ECUADOR 71
    Day 395: Friday, 8th April, 2005, Quito 71
    Day 396: Saturday, 9th April, 2005, Quito 74

GALÁPAGOS ISLANDS 81
    Day 397: Sunday, 10th April, 2005, Puerto Ayora 81
    Day 398: Monday, 11th April, 2005, Puerto Ayora 93
    Day 399: Tuesday, 12th April, 2005, NEMO I 97
    Day 400: Wednesday, 13th April, 2005, NEMO I 103
    Day 401: Thursday, 14th April, 2005, NEMO I 114
    Day 402: Friday, 15th April, 2005, NEMO I 126
    Day 403: Saturday, 16th April, 2005, NEMO I 131
    Day 404: Sunday, 17th April, 2005, NEMO I 141
    Day 405: Monday, 18th April, 2005, NEMO I 152
    Day 406: Tuesday, 19th April, 2005, Quito 162
    Day 407: Wednesday, 20th April, 2005, Flight to Miami 167

PHOTO IDENTIFICATION 172

INTRODUCTION

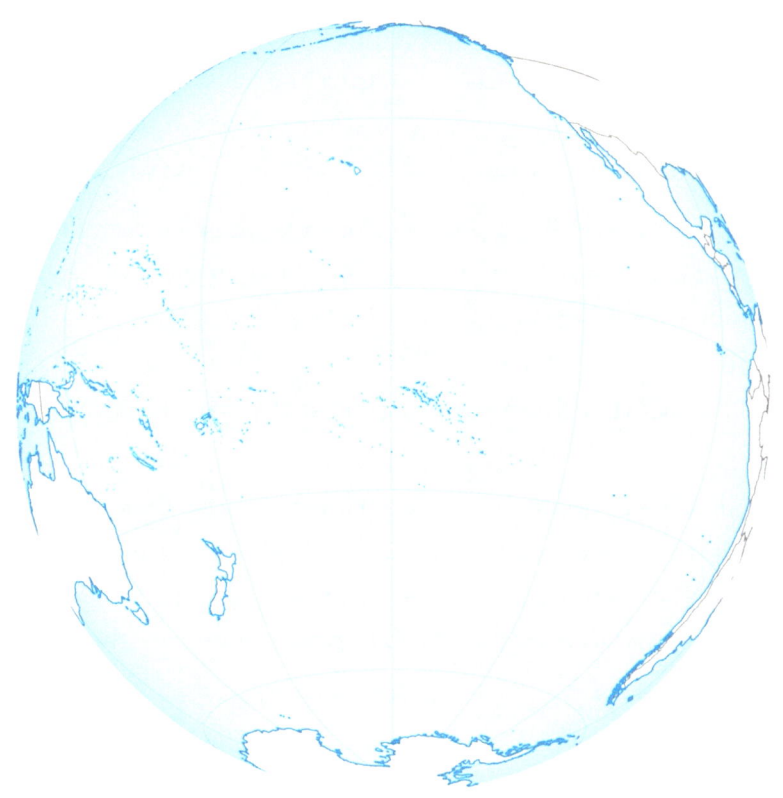

Travel Memoirs

Book 8 of 8 — OCEANIA & SOUTH AMERICA

Welcome to the final leg of our journey — the continuation of our epic round-the-world exploration, which started with Africa and the Middle East, the British Isles, India, Hong Kong & China, Southeast Asia, Australasia and now concludes with Oceania and South America.

Each volume in this 8-book series is a portal to a world brimming with diverse cultures, landscapes, and encounters. From the bustling streets of urban metropolises to the serene expanses of untouched wilderness, our quests transcended borders and boundaries, offering a tapestry of experiences woven with exhilaration, introspection, and wonder threads.

Through these memoirs, I invite you to tread the pathways we once walked, to relive the moments that shaped our odyssey across continents. Every word penned, every image captured, was a testament to the boundless spirit of exploration and the unyielding pursuit of adventure.

Join us as we unravel the tapestry of our travels, one chapter at a time. Let these tales kindle the flames of anticipation and ignite your imagination, for within these pages, the World awaits.

SCUBA diving and the natural environment

Throughout this book, I have shared glimpses of our adventures through various photos captured during our travels. Our journey through the Galapagos Islands was punctuated by immersive experiences in SCUBA diving as well as exploration of the natural environment, allowing us to explore the captivating wildlife both beneath and above the surface.

Our underwater photography endeavours began in the mesmerising depths of the Red Sea in Egypt. Initially, our equipment and skills were limited, as reflected in the quality of the photos obtained during that time. Determined to enhance our photography capabilities, we invested in upgraded equipment, including a higher-resolution camera with white balance control and an external strobe (flash). This investment significantly elevated the quality of our underwater photos, allowing us to capture the vibrant beauty of the underwater world in stunning detail.

Embarking on numerous SCUBA diving excursions allowed us to refine our photography techniques and master the nuances of underwater photography. Over time, we gradually found our rhythm, learning to maximise the potential of our equipment and adapt to the dynamic underwater environment. Each dive presented new challenges and discoveries, contributing to our growth as underwater photographers.

Our photo collection in each chapter reflects the moments we experienced firsthand. We have endeavoured to align each photo closely with the corresponding events described in the chapter text, offering readers an authentic visual narrative of our journey. While some photos may deviate slightly from the chronological sequence for formatting purposes, the essence of each image remains true to the moment captured.

Identifying the diverse marine life featured in our photos has been enriching. We have endeavoured to provide common and scientific names for each marine species, although some identifications may pose challenges due to the inherent complexities of marine life. The ever-changing nature of marine ecosystems and the remarkable abilities of certain species to adapt and camouflage add layers of intrigue to our photographic encounters.

As stewards of the ocean, we recognise the importance of conservation and responsible diving practices. Our experiences have underscored the fragility of marine ecosystems and the urgent need for conservation efforts to safeguard these invaluable habitats. Through our journey, we hope to inspire others to appreciate the beauty of the underwater world and advocate for its protection.

We invite readers to immerse themselves in our journey and engage with our content. We welcome your contributions if you spot any mislabeled species or can offer insights into unidentified marine life. Your feedback and contributions enrich our narrative, fostering a deeper connection with the wonders of the underwater world. Feel free to contact us via the book series website (https://ChrisAndSandyMorgan.com/travel/)

Join us as we delve into the ocean's depths, where every dive reveals a new chapter in our exploration of the marine realm.

The decision to go travelling

In 2002, after fourteen years of marriage, Sandy and I lived in Florida, having moved there from the Netherlands about five years previously. Initially, we intended to stay in Florida for only *a year or two*. The idea was to get out, see more of the World, and gain international experience. That might have looked good on my résumé.

While living in Florida, we built our own home. The decision to embark on our journey was fuelled by selling our house, a pivotal moment that funded our entire adventure.

Leaving America was certainly bittersweet. Florida was a great place to live. We loved the weather, the eating-out culture, the proximity to Orlando, the theme parks and other attractions, the beaches, the shopping, and so much more. I had a good job, and we enjoyed a comfortable lifestyle with plenty of disposable income. We had some wonderful friends, and it was an emotional wrench to give it all up.

However, I was ready to leave after five or six years. The weather could be oppressive in the summer. House-eating termites and nasty fire ants infested the entire state. The medical healthcare system was broken and needed replacing with a new one. There was also never any time to get out and see the country[1].

Working in IT wasn't getting any easier either. I had a good contract in Jacksonville, but that was slowly drying up, and the prospects for maintaining our lifestyle once that was gone were looking ever more in jeopardy.

The decision to leave America was also not without controversy. Sandy wasn't ready to go, but I was. That disagreement caused some tension between us over the years. The destruction of the Twin Towers in New York on 911 also influenced our decision. We had visited New York just weeks before and stood atop one of the towers. This *near miss* left its

---

[1] It's the norm in the United States for you to only get two weeks of holiday each year.

mark on us. It made us consider our mortality and everything we still wanted to achieve in our lifetimes.

As we contemplated our journey back to Europe and the desire to explore Australia, the obstacle of expensive flight tickets seemed insurmountable. Little did we know that a serendipitous discovery awaited — one that would change the course of our travel plans entirely.

When we first made that mental decision, the next thing to consider was where to go. We wanted to go back home to Europe. The expectation was to have plenty of money from the proceeds of the sale of the house. That expectation meant there was never any pressure to return to work. I had always wanted to visit my cousin, Marie (Ree-Ree), in Australia, so we decided to first go to Australia for a visit: a detour on the way back to Europe.

Looking at an atlas or globe showed that Australia was not exactly *on the way* from Florida to Europe. It was in the opposite direction and quite a significant detour. Worse still, buying flight tickets from Florida to Australia and then from Australia to Europe was prohibitively expensive. The idea to visit my relatives down under seemed doomed from the get-go.

A serendipitous discovery awaited me when I stumbled upon the concept of a *round-the-world ticket* in a travel forum. The discussions immediately captured my interest. An RTW ticket was a particular type of flight (or series of flights, to be more accurate) that allowed us to circumnavigate the globe. It was essentially a flight from London to Australia and back to London again, but we also got to take a couple of extra flights within each continent we passed through. Other than the initial departure date, which we had to set in stone, the timing of each flight leg was otherwise flexible — provided we completed the entire journey within 12 months.

Instead of a couple thousand dollars each for flights from London to Melbourne and then again for the return journey, an RTW ticket for both of us would cost just €5000. The RTW ticket also allowed us to plan where to stop and spend time. We could create an entire itinerary for what would otherwise be a fraction of the price of booking each of the legs separately.

Suddenly, the trip to Australia was on the cards again. Better yet, we could also decide on other countries to visit. Best of all was that we had a whole year to play with. What started as a quick trip to Australia and then onward to Europe ultimately developed through a year's worth of planning into a much more epic journey.

Where to travel to

While planning the trip, the list of places we *absolutely must see* kept growing and growing. Since we had money to spend and no set timeline to adhere to other than the 12-month journey-completion time requirement, we thought, *why not go big?* Truthfully, *I* was responsible for continually expanding the list of countries to visit. The house sale eventually netted us around $40,000 to play with. As it turned out, the entire RTW journey cost around €35,000 (around $40,000).

RTW airline tickets weren't widely known when we were researching the trip. Two main airline alliances operated these tickets: *One World* and *Star Alliance*. One World included British Airways, Qantas, American Airlines, Cathay Pacific, and others. I desperately wanted to include Easter Island in the list of must-visit places. Only one airline flew there, LATAM, a major Latin American operator based in Chile. LATAM was a member of the One World Alliance. That fact largely dictated purchasing a One World RTW ticket instead of a Star Alliance version. The rest of the itinerary was ultimately constructed around that initial decision, as the destinations serviced by those airlines that comprised the One World alliance dictated our options.

From the initial idea to departure, it was about a year. That gave me ample time to develop many destinations and route permutations to research. I joined and participated in various discussion forums, read loads of guidebooks, spoke to many other travellers, and researched the entire endeavour to within an inch of its life.

Throughout the year of planning, the list of countries and our chosen route underwent multiple transformations, reflecting the evolving nature of our aspirations. I had numerous different routes that were in contention for the final choice. For example, the initial plan was to visit Russia first and then take the Trans-Siberian Express to Mongolia and China. With this initial choice of direction and route in mind, Sandy and I even took some Russian and Mandarin lessons with the full expectation that English wouldn't serve us well in those countries. Sandy was also never thrilled with the idea of 7 full days on a train. Eventually, we had to give up on going to Russia since no One World airline serviced it.

Other places I initially had high hopes of squeezing in were Japan, Korea, Malaysia, Iceland, Peru, Brazil, and Mexico. I would get excited each time about adding another potential destination to the country list. That excitement faded once it became clear we'd need to spend less time elsewhere to make it possible. It was a constant juggling act and a veritable roller-coaster ride of mixed emotions.

Eventually, we decided to break up the journey into multiple legs. The first leg would be Africa and the Middle East, which would take about four months. Then we bought a second-hand camper van and spent another few months touring the British Isles. These two trips were a learning exercise for the main thrust of the journey: a separate 8-month global circumnavigation, for which we bought a special RTW airline ticket.

What to take with us

By the time we left Florida for London, we had done all the research and figured out how and where we would travel. We would be backpacking, so everything we needed to live on for months had to be organised precisely and packed into a light backpack to be worn and taken anywhere comfortably. Getting the contents of our kit right was a challenging feat. It required significant planning and consideration. When we carried our entire house on our backs, we became fastidious and paranoid about how much everything weighed. Every gram was hard fought for. It was incredible how many ways there were to save weight. I even heard stories of people drilling holes into their toothbrushes to save weight. We weren't that neurotic, but we were probably not that far behind.

Another consideration that required plenty of planning was staying healthy while travelling. We would be visiting places where access to health care might not be as readily available as we were used to. As such, we had to take half a pharmacy's worth of first aid gear and have a whole battery of vaccinations. And then there was the stockpile of different anti-malarial tablets to cater for the various varieties of malaria zones we would pass through.

Sandy and I are avid photographers, and I wanted to document every aspect of the trip as far as possible by writing about it. Consequently, in addition to the backpacks, all our clothing for all weathers, and our significant medical kit, we also had to find space and weight allowance for cameras, lenses, a laptop, charging cables, etc. Everything needed to sustain us for several months, including the backpack, had to come in at 20 Kg (44 lbs) or less. The 20 Kg limitation was due to the anticipated luggage weight allowance for some of the smaller flights to out-of-the-way places along the route. Anything more than 20 kg, and we would risk certain airlines refusing to take us. There was also the problem of carrying that much weight on our backs for days.

By the time we made it to London, our jumping-off point for the trip, we had finally settled on all the light-weight high-performance clothing, footwear, backpacks, electronics, cameras, medical kit and padlocks to keep it all safe and secure in youth hostels, and everything else to sustain us. We decided to test it all and booked a long weekend via train to a nondescript, low-budget hostel in the middle of Paris. The idea was to see how well we could manage using nothing more than what we had decided to cram into our backpacks.

The Paris trip was a success. All the research had paid off. The biggest problem we had was the cold. We designed the RTW journey for warm-weather clothing. We had a follow-the-sun strategy that ensured we would always travel in warm climates — crossing the equator at certain times of the year to avoid winter in that hemisphere. This strategy resulted in a substantial weight saving since warm-weather clothing was lighter than cold-weather clothing. However, Paris in January was not the place to be when you only had thin fabrics and no heavy jacket.

Our final kit selection remained a perpetual work in progress. It was only after hitting the road that we grasped the essentials and could identify items we could comfortably discard.

There was an adage that was always good advice to new travellers: Double the money you take and half the backpack contents. I ultimately understood how true this was only after being on the road. You'd be amazed at the number of things you *think* you must have but never need or use.

Documenting the journey

I wanted to ensure that I recorded every trip detail for posterity. Fortunately, I was a bit of a data freak. Collecting data was something that came naturally to me. I also enjoyed communicating using the written word, so writing blogs or travel journals seemed like it would be a fun thing to do.

I meticulously wrote about daily events leading up to and during the journey. I sat down at the laptop every night to record the day's events in a daily blog. Each day's journal entry could be anywhere from a single page, summarising the main events to numerous pages going into lots of detail.

Because we had moved from Florida to the UK and had some weeks before we started, including the test trip to Paris, I was able to hone my blog-writing skills before we boarded the first plane. Capturing some of the pre-departure perspectives was also a good idea.

Between the pre-departure blogs and the daily chronicles of our journey, I amassed over 400 entries, collectively comprising over 520,000 words. If I published that collection of works in a standard 6" x 9" book format, it would be around 1,500 pages long — or eight full-length novels.

This book presents the unabridged versions of the travel blogs captured during our tour around the British Isles.

In addition to the blog writing, I also captured lots of data in various spreadsheets. Things like where we stayed each night, how the overall budget broke down, our daily expenses, etc., were all meticulously documented. Here are some of the things I recorded in my tracking spreadsheets:

- Flights
- Luxuries
- Diving
- Visas
- Total spend per country
- ATM withdrawals
- Traveller's cheques cashed in

It was all laid out in my spreadsheets.

Adding a personal touch to our documentation, we meticulously purchased souvenirs, sending them home when our backpacks became too heavy. We found at least one thing — sometimes many more than just one — in every country we passed through. When our backpacks became too heavy, we'd find a post office and dispatch a few items we'd collected back to the UK for safekeeping.

TAHITI

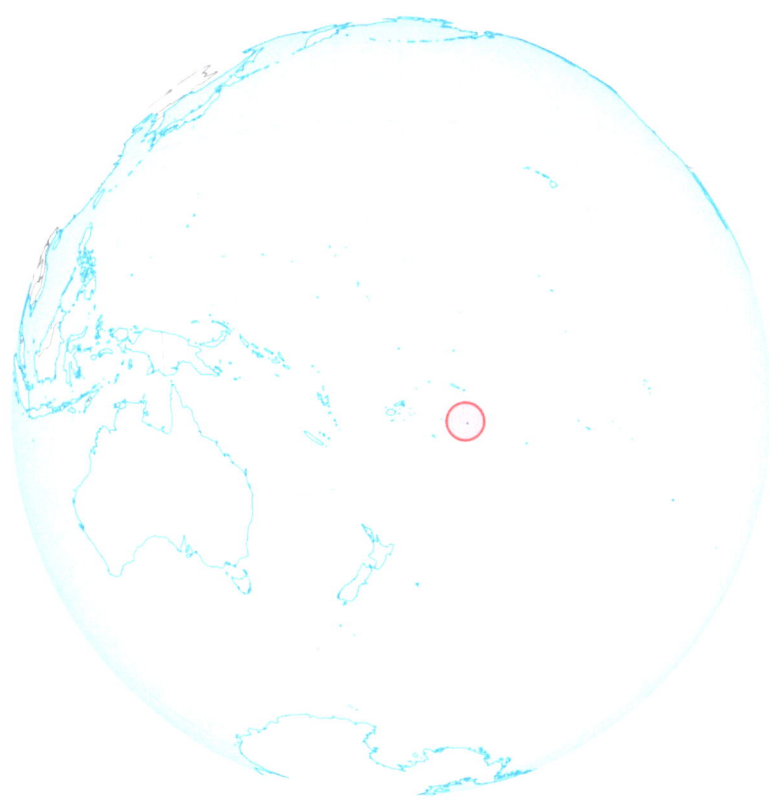

Day 387: Wednesday, 30th March, 2005, Papeete

It was a little bit hurried this morning since we didn't get up particularly early, but we still had to vacate the room by ten o'clock to avoid a late checkout fee. I doubted the rather friendly owners would have levied such a fee, but it was enough of an incentive anyway for us to get things moving. We decided to boil some eggs to take with us on the road for breakfast. The plan was to stop somewhere on the way to the airport to buy some rolls. The hostel's free food shelf was the lucky recipient of several of our bits and pieces that we decided not to take with us on the afternoon flight from Auckland to Tahiti. Naturally, I whipped out the laptop for one last whiz on the Internet to exchange e-mails.

A bit of a nasty going away present awaited me on the car's windscreen when I started loading it this morning. Although I was parked in a spot where I was allowed to park, I was hit with a NZ$40 (€23.20) fine for facing the wrong direction. Facing the wrong bloody direction? What the hell was that all about? Thanks, New Zealand; I really needed that! Ordinarily, such an annoyance would have hurtled me into a nasty mood for the rest of the day, but I did my best to laugh that one off. At the very least, it made for an amusing tale to tell in the years to come. That's it, Chris, you keep telling yourself that.

After packing and bidding farewell to the friendly owners of the Aloe Lodge hostel, we set off to find a supermarket. The same supermarket we visited yesterday had its own car park, even though we had to spend more than NZ$5 (€2.50) for two hours of free parking. We picked up some fresh bread rolls and a few other titbits from there, and with a few directions from the parking attendant, we were finally off to the airport.

Actually, we first sat in the car in the car park and ate the boiled eggs and rolls. Somewhat naively, once underway, I assumed I'd have to follow the signs to the rental car return bay. Unfortunately, however, our rental agency didn't have a stand at the airport, despite the rental agreement telling us to return the car to the airport. We needed to be just outside the airport. We could only find it with the help of an idle taxi driver.

We paid the deposit for the rental car using a credit card. With this being our last day in New Zealand, I didn't want the city parking authorities to follow our electronic trail and hit us with an even bigger penalty for not paying the ridiculous *facing the wrong bloody direction fine* we just landed.

The young girl operating the desk at the rental agency was sympathetic about the parking ticket. She thought it was just as ludicrous as I did. Fortunately, I could pay the fine directly to them, and they would settle with the city authorities. They did that quite a bit. She gave me a receipt showing that the fine had been paid, so that should be the end of the matter.

We jumped onto the rental agency's shuttle to the airport. Once we arrived, we had to return to collect some things we'd forgotten to take out of the car. Doh! We took those mishaps in our stride now.

The queues at the airport for our flight were quite long. Again, we took it all in our stride, just tagging on to the end of the one we thought was correct. I say *thought was correct* since the flight number printed in our flight coupon wasn't displayed anywhere on the screens. The queue we joined, however, was for a flight bound for our destination with the exact departure and arrival times, so I was confident we were in the right place. That turned out to be correct in the end.

All the usual airport formalities were now so second nature to us that we barely acknowledged them anymore. We leisurely stopped for a snack in the departure hall. When we reached the gate, the remaining passengers were already boarding the flight. Sandy had asked for an aisle seat at check-in, and we were happy to find that we were placed in the bulkhead seats right next to the emergency exit — so we'd be the first sucked out if it failed.

Our Airbus A330 was practically new and most comfortable. That Qantas flight was a codeshare with Air Tahiti Nui. Since Tahiti was French Polynesian, all the staff on board spoke French.

We lost another two hours to the time zone fairy when we arrived in Papeete, Tahiti's capital. In addition to that problem, we would lose an entire day from the calendar when arriving on Easter Island because of passing over the International Date Line. That's why there will be a gap in the log entries for 1st March. Initially, I had tried to plan that we passed through the International Date Line on 21st March so that I could skip my birthday and thus be a year younger. If my birthday never happened, I wouldn't have aged another year, right? I'm sure that logic is sound. However, that plan was another casualty lost to the pregnancy fairy.

I had some misgivings about our intended arrival in Papeete. Tahiti was known throughout the backpacker community as a costly and budget-busting destination. I'd also heard tales of a lack of independent tourist infrastructure at the airport, which had supposedly thwarted many an independent traveller upon arrival. Fortunately, we at least had a car, and our one night's accommodation was already sorted.

It was well into the night when we landed at Papeete. The beautifully adorned girls handing each arriving passenger a small flower to tuck behind their ear was a nice touch, as was the three-person band of musicians playing traditional music as we lined up for the immigration formalities.

After collecting our bags, there was a very long queue at the green channel to clear customs, so we walked over to the empty red channel to hand in the two oranges we still had. Unfortunately, after removing our oranges, our man sent us back to the green channel queue again. Oh well, nothing ventured, nothing gained. It worked sometimes.

The arrivals hall at Tahiti was a surprise. It was much bigger than I had earlier been led to believe. There was even a staffed information counter. We swiftly located the Avis rental car desk to collect our car, but I had an issue with the French-speaking woman about the number of free kilometre allowances that came with the rental agreement.

I had made the reservation over the Internet and had the foresight to screenshot the page displaying the agreement, which clearly stated we had an allowance of 84 km (52 miles). Mrs French, however, was insistent it was only to be fifty km (31 miles). There are well over two hundred kilometres of potential roads to explore on Tahiti. When I returned the car, I didn't relish paying a small fortune in additional kilometre charges, so I whipped out the laptop and showed her the booking screenshot. She was insistent until she noticed the reservation was for one day and a couple of hours instead of the stock one-day term. She told me not to worry and would sort it out in the system. I had my doubts, but with communications being what they were, it seemed fruitless to pursue the matter further.

The people at the information desk were invaluable in searching for a budget place to sleep for the night. We already had the reservation with the one place I've been exchanging e-mails with. However, I didn't see the harm in shopping around a bit anyway to make sure we weren't being ripped off. As it turned out, they rang around all the budget pensions and ended up with the one place we had already booked. If nothing else, it proved we weren't being overcharged for what we had already booked. Everywhere else was fully booked. I guess that at least demonstrated it wasn't a good idea to show up on Tahiti unprepared.

As I talked to the information desk girl about the room rate and how to get there, a representative from the lodgings we had booked over the Internet appeared as if by magic and gave us directions. How was that for service?

We drove out of the muggy airport and towards Papeete with our brand-new French car. It wasn't far — about the length of the runway again. The road signs were similar to those we'd have expected to find in France. My first impression at that point was that Tahiti was nothing like I expected it to be. The image I always had of Tahiti was of tropical, palm-lined, sandy beaches with beach hut accommodations raised over the water's surface and a boardwalk linking all the huts to the mainland. Unfortunately, our budget would not extend to such honeymoon-like luxuries.

So far, we'd seen developed, if slightly worn and a little run down, roads that linked small towns. As we entered Papeete, it immediately struck us that almost everywhere was closed, with shutters in front of all the shop windows. That didn't bode well for our designs on grabbing a bite to eat for the night. We managed to spot one restaurant that still looked open for business, so we found a spot to park the car and walked over. The restaurant owner spoke good English and seemed like a nice guy. The food was excellent. The bill came to FCP3,500 (€31,82). I thought that wasn't bad for Tahiti.

Now fed and somewhat rested from the flight, we set to locate our lodgings, a privately run pension. It was supposed to be just a couple of streets up into town, but that didn't stop us driving up and down a couple of times before we located the correct turnoff. Our capacity for getting lost was by now legendary. The main problem was that none of the street signs were legible. They were all bleached out, so we couldn't read the letters. The writing was always barely decipherable. We finally found our road exactly where it was supposed to be based on the map on the little brochure we picked up from the airport. I parked the car and rang the bell on the gate outside.

After several minutes, a young girl came out to greet us. This charming little Polynesian-looking teenager had clearly just woken up. It took several minutes before she was fully conscious and coherent. Luckily, she spoke relatively good English (certainly much better than our French), and we all sat around the patio table for a few minutes going over the formalities.

The room rate was FCP7,990 (€72,64) after tax, but that was for the room without an en-suite. We picked up a few suggestions of where to go to kill time tomorrow. Communication was a bit broken at times, but we somehow muddled through. The room had no air conditioning, but a floor-standing fan would suffice. We were clearly about to fall asleep, so we freshened up and went to bed.

Day 388: Thursday, 31st March, 2005, Papeete

As predicted, we missed the complimentary breakfast this morning. The young girl who met us last night worked there all by herself seven days a week. I did ask if it would be possible to extend the breakfast hours, but she didn't have the time or energy to accommodate the request. At eight o'clock that morning, when the breakfast table was already being cleared, our body clocks still thought it was six o'clock, so it was no surprise we missed out. We both slept relatively well — except for Sandy, who found the bed too hard and the fan's noise rather annoying (she always did).

After re-loading the car and bidding farewell to our overworked young hostess, we drove back into town to find the tourist information office and a map of the island. Tahiti's main island landmass is about 60 km (37 miles) in diameter, with a smaller 15 km (9 miles) diameter landmass jutting up to it. The tourist map I was given looked very nice but was useless as a navigational aid. With only today to explore the island, I asked where we might go to relax on a beach and perhaps take in some snorkelling. Communication was once again haphazard. I was only getting very brief and monosyllabic responses. We decided to throw caution to the wind and explore ourselves.

We were headed toward Punaauia, where we could apparently go snorkelling. There was just one main ring road encircling the entire island. That was depicted on the map. However, we passed through more roads and road systems in each town that the map didn't show. Before checking out the beach, we thought we'd take in the Musée de Tahiti et des Îles, also known as Te Fare Manaha Museum, which, according to our tourist map, was just about the only thing in Punaauia. That was where the map started to fail us terribly.

We drove around looking for what might look like a museum but were eventually forced to stop at what turned out to be the City Hall. A pleasant guy there told us the museum was not worth the effort. He suggested we go straight to the beach instead. Large hotel chains privately owned many of the beaches on Tahiti. Those were the ones we conjured when thinking of Tahiti. Like I said before, we wouldn't be seeing any of those.

The public beach that we found was exactly that — a public beach. It wasn't massive and certainly not worth the effort. It was located next to a boat dock. The water wasn't clear, although it was relatively warm.

Having seen so many picturesque beaches in so many tropical locations, we were spoiled now to the point of really needing to see something spectacular before our blood got pumping. Just because we were on Tahiti, that didn't cut the mustard.

Several hundred meters from the shore, a sand bank encircled the island, creating a lagoon nearly all the way around. The worthwhile stuff to snorkel after was out by the barrier of that bank. That was too far for comfort, so we never went swimming or snorkelling.

A dive school was adjacent to the boat dock, so we went over to see about going out for a dive instead for the afternoon. Indeed, after a quick chat with the guy there, it seemed like a decent way to spend the afternoon. Fortunately, it would be a shallow dive. I was technically not supposed to dive and fly within the same twenty-four-hour period, but I was willing to be flexible given the limited depths. After all, I didn't get to Tahiti every day, did I?

The cost of the single dive was FCP 4,800 (€43,64). That didn't seem like a massive price for French Polynesia, so I signed up for a single afternoon dive.

With a couple of hours to kill, we stopped at the McDonald's just next to the boat dock for the most expensive fast food we've yet experienced. Still, it had to be much cheaper than anywhere else. Just as we sat to eat, the weather started to turn. What just a couple of minutes ago had been a mostly clear and blue sky had now developed into something more ominous. A dark cloud was forming from above the island's land mass. That dark cloud spent the next half an hour emptying itself directly on top of us. As a result, I worried about the underwater visibility of my afternoon dive.

Not only did the rain clear up, but there was no evidence of it having rained after half an hour. That was reminiscent of the Florida summers we used to enjoy. We'd see a torrential downpour of near-horizontal driving rain almost every afternoon during the summer. Thirty minutes later, there'd be no evidence of it having rained.

Of course, Sandy had to skip the diving because she was pregnant. She contented herself with sitting under the tropical sun with one of her books.

There were about eight people on the boat altogether. It was a very nice shallow dive, with an average depth of just around ten metres. Visibility was crystal clear, which was a bonus. The bottom composition of hard corals was interesting enough, even though there were few fish compared to other dive locations in different countries I'd explored on this trip. A couple of small turtles kept us all interested for a while, but the three sleeping black-tipped sharks resting on the seabed right towards the end of the dive thrilled us all.

I took many photos but never saw anything specific to add to my all-time underwater best-of photo album. It was an average dive that served well to kill some time this afternoon.

Once the dive boat returned to the dock, things were very relaxed. We spent an hour or two just sitting in the sun, trying to dry everything off. Some of the divers were doing a written SCUBA diving test, so we repackaged our bags and tidied up slowly. We nearly made off inadvertently without paying, but one of the dive instructors ran after our car to remind us.

When we first arrived at the airport, the pension representative who came to give us directions tried to tell us where to go to get a bite to eat. He was challenging to understand. We never found where he was pointing us, but it had something to do with what we thought was the word *car* or *key*. He seemed to be telling us that we could get food from a car — perhaps like a food vendor serving from the side of a van or something. In the light of day today, we decided to head over to where he had directed us to see what it was all about.

We found it in the end. He had probably been trying to tell us to go to the quay. Indeed, there was a dock or quay on the waterfront near the city centre where a dozen or more travelling food stalls were setting up mobile restaurants. Each van specialised in a different type of food and came complete with tables and chairs outside. It was a nightly ritual in

Tahiti. Plenty of people were slowly starting to assemble for their evening meals. I was amazed to see so many young children accompanying their parents on holiday there. Every fourth or fifth tourist was toting a small child or a pushchair.

A bandstand housed musicians playing amplified music. Soft lighting completed the relaxing atmosphere. The sun slowly set, and a gentle, warm sea breeze wafted. It might not have been the quintessential Tahiti-style ocean-beach-hut setting we conjured in our minds, but it was a pleasant atmosphere.

The stall we eventually chose was roasting a small cow over an open pit barbeque. The meal was tremendous and cost us FCP1,000 (€9,10).

Sitting under the soft lighting and listening to Polynesian music was pleasant enough for a while, but boredom finally drove us back to the airport to return the car. Luckily, we caught the Avis clerk before she closed the office for a few hours. She calculated the final tally for the one-day rental to be FCP5,877 (€53,43), all-inclusive. That was less than we had expected, but I wasn't complaining.

That evening's meal meant breaking into one of the bank notes I was holding back for my complete collection of Tahiti currency, so I exchanged one of my £20 notes to restock. We would have been well under our budget for Tahiti had I not collected one of every banknote, but the FCP10,000 note alone is already worth €90,10. I'd given us a €250 budget, but with the banknote collection, we spent a total of €363.

We were still a couple hours ahead of the check-in staff, so we found a place to sit near an electrical outlet. I'd at least then be able to continue to write my journals.

The boarding announcement eventually came. We walked across the tarmac to yet another plane bound for yet another new destination.

EASTER ISLAND

Day 389: Saturday, 2nd April, 2005, Hanga Roa

Our light to Easter Island was only about half full. We were lucky enough to get a three-seat centre row all to ourselves. I tried to get horizontal as soon as the seatbelt sign was dimmed. Sandy eventually moved into another seat, and I did my best to get as much sleep as possible. I would have succeeded if it weren't for the excited Russian-speaking woman sitting in the row behind me mouthing off throughout the flight. During the five-hour flight, I may have caught an hour's worth of cumulative sleep.

The plane taxied in a straight line for a long time before coming to a halt after landing. Easter Island has a runway long enough to serve as a backup and emergency runway for NASA's space shuttle. I'd estimate that only about half the passengers disembarked the plane, with the rest continuing to Santiago. Santiago, Chile, and Papeete, Tahiti, were the only two places connecting with Easter Island by air. The tiny special territory of Chile in the far east of the Pacific Ocean is the remotest inhabited island on the planet.

We stepped out onto the tarmac with our completed landing cards at the ready. In doing so, I realised a dream long in the making. Even though I was very tired from the flight, I still managed to catch myself quietly chuckling internally for having finally reached this new milestone. That was another life's to-do list item that I could now cross off the list — few remain. I would saviour the moment briefly and let it sink in over the coming days.

Our first impressions of Easter Island were that it was a subtropical remote island with few trees but lots of low-lying tropical vegetation and grassland reminiscent of Thailand and Cambodia.

Immigration formalities were particularly slow, but we weren't bothered since we were the first off the plane. The luggage belt was encircled with accommodation booths, most of which were staffed by people trying to catch our attention. One such booth had the name of the pension that I had chosen from our guidebook. We spoke briefly with the nice man sitting in it after collecting our luggage. He tried to tell me there were a lot of tourists on the island and that he wanted to charge us US $35 (€26.92) for the room, as opposed to the US $30 (€23.08) listed in the guidebook. I told him it didn't look hectic, which was true. His heart couldn't have been in it. He quickly buckled and gave us the going rate of US $30 (€23.08).

He then summoned a taxi to take us just around the corner to the pension. The very old driver drove very slowly. I don't think he even got out of first gear. Judging by the state of the car, it may not have had any other functional gear.

The pension we arrived at looked a little ragged and was overgrown with vegetation. The room was a bit musty, and the bed was firm, though certainly nothing we couldn't handle.

The real killer was the absence of any kitchen or cooking facilities. I queried him about that. He tried to feed me a line of crap about this being a new system on the island with no kitchen facilities in the pensions. That blatant lie was so transparent that I think he felt embarrassed. He suggested another pension just around the corner, so we got back into the taxi again. As it turned out, that second place was right next door around the corner and looked very similar from the outside. It had a kitchen, and our room had an en-suite bathroom. With the aid of our YHA cards, we secured the same US $30 (€23.08) room rate for each of our four nights on the islands.

The house owner didn't speak English, but we'd managed so far with just a spattering of Spanish and a liberal dose of body language. I was sure we'd continue to manage somehow. Sandy went to catch up on the sleep she lost during the red-eye flight, and I went for a stroll into town.

The small town of Hanga Roa is the only settlement on the island, save for the odd house dotted here and there. Pretty much all 3800[2] inhabitants of the island lived there permanently, although you wouldn't think there were that many people to see the place. There were just a few streets, and the small town was quite dispersed. In total, the town was little more than four square kilometres. It's an economically challenged place. Almost all of Easter Island's revenue was derived from tourism. Everyone there relied either directly or indirectly on the tourism trade.

The pickings were slim as far as shopping was concerned. Although a few shops were scattered about, the choice of goods on offer was minimal. There were a couple of general stores and several souvenir outlets selling carved wooden curios and lava stone carvings of the standing Moai. The enigmatic standing Moai statues made Easter Island

---

[2] At the time of this writing, in 2024, Easter Island's population is closer to 8000.

significant so disproportionate to its size. There was just one petrol station, bank, and post office in town. The electricity went out at certain times. The people there, however, were friendly and laid back. Although English wasn't commonly spoken, communication wasn't too difficult for basic needs. All we needed was a sense of adventure and an open mind. We had both in abundance.

Hang Roa sits in the southwest corner of the roughly triangular-shaped island, formed from the conjunction of three long-since-extinct volcanoes. Much of the island was covered in volcanic rock from past lava flows, with grassland stretching out over the flows. Igneous rock could be found lying everywhere.

There were a few options for getting around. The guidebook suggested it would take three days to walk around the island comfortably, but there were taxis that we could bargain with, too. The preferred method was renting a Suzuki four-by-four Jeep. I noted several of those driving around as I wandered through town.

The going rate for a jeep was between US $50 (€38.46) and US $70 (€53.85) per day. I popped into the small tourism office to inquire about renting one for the duration. The young girl there spoke passable English but told me I had to visit one of the shops displaying a Jeep rental sign. They are all the same price, so it shouldn't have mattered where I chose to rent from. Strangely, for a tourism office, she had no maps of the island.

The tourism office was right near the waterfront. That was where I saw my first standing Moai. In fact, there were a couple of them there, and they were indeed curious-looking. One of the smaller volcanoes on the island was the quarry from which the figurehead statues were carved out of the rock face. Somehow, those stone figures had been moved around the island to be erected where they currently stand. However, during past political unrest, many had been toppled over. Some of them were thought to be nearly three thousand years old. That raised many questions about who built them and how they were moved. Many theories abound as to whom, why and what, but just as many disagreements.

I noted some diving operators near the waterfront area, so I considered diving while on the island.

On my way back to the pension, I also stopped in at what looked like an artist's market, where several rows of market stalls were adorned with the local artist's wares. The prices listed were not particularly cheap. I didn't want to get into a haggling match without first learning more about the local customs, so I didn't ask for prices as I walked around.

Before I set foot on the island, I had already decided to rent a Jeep, so I popped into one of the shops displaying a Jeep rental sign and tried to negotiate with the Spanish-speaking woman there. Even though neither of us spoke each other's language, we managed well enough and agreed that I would return in an hour to collect my jeep for the arranged price of US $200 (€153.85) for the four days. The woman was friendly and seemed laid back about the whole thing.

Back at the pension, Sandy was still drifting in and out of sleep. It didn't take me long to doze off myself after putting my head down. It was several hours later that we both roused again. We shook ourselves awake to walk back into town and collect our Jeep.

A relatively clean-looking Jeep was parked outside the little shop where I had spoken with the lovely lady earlier, but the shop itself was shut. In fact, from what we could tell, all the shops were closed. Might that be due to an afternoon siesta?

In the meantime, hunger was tightening its grip on us, so we wandered around until we found a small restaurant. As with almost every other place we'd seen, nothing was posted in English. We did our best to order what we thought were a plain chicken sandwich and a plain steak sandwich for lunch. What came out was close enough. As we ate, a couple of young Japanese tourists wandered onto the restaurant's front deck. They were clearly in the same boat as us. They ultimately ordered what they wanted by pointing to what we were eating. We talked to them about how they would move around the island and even offered to share our Jeep with them. Although extremely grateful for the offer, they decided to jump onto one of the many guided tours that departed daily from Hanga Roa.

By now, the Jeep rental shop was open again, so we went over to collect our four-by-four. It was rough and ready but seemed sturdy enough to meet our needs for the next few days. It has just under half a tank of fuel. The woman tried to tell me to return it with a similar amount; at least, that's what I assumed.

Unless I was very much mistaken, she also told me to leave it parked at the airport, just a few minutes away on foot. We had to leave the keys in the ignition when we left. I thought that was very trusting of her. Then again, who'd be stupid enough to steal a Jeep when you lived in a small village on a tiny island in the middle of the world's largest ocean?

Even though the island was small, our driving progress would be slow, with dirt tracks and off-road terrain. It was anyone's guess how long the less-than-half-full tank of fuel would last. I decided we should drive to the petrol station to get some petrol. That sounded simple, didn't it? Not on Easter Island!

We arrived at the island's only filling station. There was just the single ancient pump with an attendant sitting beside it. Several other vehicles on both sides of the pump were waiting to get fuel, so I went inside to browse around. It was a sleepy, laid-back atmosphere with half-empty shelves. I bought and paid for several water bottles before it hit me. Nobody was getting any fuel pumped. I asked the cashier what the problem was. She told me (mimed would be more accurate) that the island's electricity was off. The pumps wouldn't start working until six o'clock. Since it was now ten to six, sitting and waiting for a while didn't seem like a hardship, so that's what we did.

It didn't take long before quite a few vehicles of varying description were waiting for the power to come back on so that they could refuel. Kids were now running around and playing between all the cars. Sandy, with her usual magnetic attraction to children, had a great time feeding some of them with snacks we had previously stocked up on.

We sat there for an hour and a half before the power finally kicked in. We could tell from the relaxed and laid-back attitude of everyone else at the pump that it was all part and parcel of everyday life on Easter Island. Nobody cared about the wait. When the power came on, they slowly got into their vehicles, and the pump boy tried to put fuel into as many as he could as quickly as possible. I put US $20 (€15.38) into the tank, filling it completely.

We had planned on exploring the island, but it was now getting dark, so we drove off in search of a restaurant instead. We found a place near the waterfront. That turned out to be a mistake. The food was not great there. The German owner did, however, give us a much more favourable exchange rate for paying in US dollars. He explained that we would be better off withdrawing some local currency from the island's only ATM. That way, we would get something like 650 Chilean Pesos for every US dollar, as opposed to the relatively poor 500 all the shops and restaurants gave. Everyone accepted US dollars and Chilean Pesos, but we always received Chilean Pesos back as change.

Day 390: Sunday, 3rd April, 2005, Hanga Roa

We both had an extremely restless night. The guidebook had already warned us of the island's problem of noisy dogs, but I was unprepared for just how persistent they were.

I could usually tolerate noise whilst I slept, but those dogs just would not stop barking all through the entire frigging night. There was one very large and very loud dog in particular tied up in a pen just across the street that seemed to start barking every few minutes or so (or rather, only stopped barking for a few seconds every hour or so). Each time it sounded off, the entire neighbourhood of a dozen or more dogs joined in like an involuntary chain reaction. The resulting cacophony of howling continued for five to ten minutes at a time.

I couldn't understand why the dog owners allowed that incessant barking to continue hour after hour through the night.

Adding to the near-constant shrill of the dogs barking was the ritual crowing of all the town's roosters every hour on the hour. Colonel Sanders needed to get his ass over to Easter Island pronto.

It wasn't just the neighbourhood animals to blame. Oh no! All the discothèques got into full swing from about one or two o'clock. They continued blaring all through the night. I could hear the din thumping out over the town each time the wind blew in our direction.

At one point, I opened the laptop to see what time it was. I was amazed the loud music was still pumping away at four in the morning. Throw in a lot of rustling from all the vegetation overgrowing the house whenever the wind blew, along with all the wind chimes the owners hung up everywhere, and the inescapable symphony was complete. I probably would have slept better if a pneumatic drill was stuck in high gear next to the bed to drown out all the noise.

Breakfast that morning, what there was of it, was laid out on the table in the dining room cum living room. I managed a banana and a glass of juice, but that was about it. Without any cereals or anything warm, there was nothing there that took my fancy. Sandy contented herself with just a banana. Food was often our Achilles' heel during our travels.

We took the bottles of water I picked up from the petrol station yesterday and set out with cameras and a map of the island to explore what was to explore.

The one place on the island Sandy especially wanted to see was the volcano, from where the Moai statues were harvested. We got into the Jeep and headed for the island's northeast corner.

The roads on the island and the roads depicted on our map agreed by and large, but there were some glaring inaccuracies. In fact, no two maps we'd seen agreed on which roads existed, where they met up and in which direction they went when they did exist. You'd think that creating an accurate map would not be difficult for a landmass this small and with just a handful of roads to contend with. For whatever reason, it was a challenge beyond even the most capable mapmakers. Perhaps the cartographers came but were driven away prematurely by the noise of the dogs and thus had to subsequently make things up to get the job done.

There were just a couple of paved roads leading away from Hanga Roa. After wasting half an hour trying to find the paved road, we followed one along the Southeast coastline. We had initially found some dirt tracks while trying to follow the map. Still, at least that gave me time to figure out how to operate the four-wheel drive mechanism. Driving on the paved roads was much more comfortable after figuring out how to disengage the four-wheel drive.

There were many Moai statues along the Southeast coastline. Almost all of them had been toppled. The carved igneous rock figures lie face down on the ground — casualties of Easter Island's history and past embattlements.

We passed several spots where tour guides were leading tour groups around. For some bizarre reason, all the tour groups departed simultaneously, followed the same route around the island and generally travelled at the same pace. The net result was that all the tour groups piled up together at all the stops along the way. That was another one of those Easter Island oddities. I thought it was an insane tactic to follow, but perhaps insanity was one of the by-products of the sleep deprivation from all the nocturnal dogs. Whatever the reason, we did our best to avoid them where possible.

The magical qualities of Easter Island were somewhat displaced when a group of rowdy Germans came trampling through at high speed, all armed with camcorders. We quietly stepped aside to let them proceed unhindered.

The volcano we sought was not hard to find. The island was formed from the lava flows of one of three volcanoes, each readily visible on the horizon. We parked the Jeep as close as possible and started walking up the grassy slopes of the volcano's caldera.

Dotted around the rim were numerous standing Moai. Higher up, there was a section known as the nursery, where several Moai could still be found where they were left, in various stages of being carved and excavated from the rock face.

The Moai ranged in size from just a few metres at the small end to the largest at over 20 m (65 ft) in length. They were carved right out of the porous igneous rock from the side of the volcano. We scaled the outer rim and then down to its lowest point to find a swamp on the inside with yet more Moai statues standing majestically on the inside of the caldera.

There were plenty of statues inside and outside of the volcano's crater. Many had been toppled and were in varying stages of overgrowth from the surrounding shrub and grassland.

All the climbing took its toll on Sandy, so she sat and rested on the rim's lowest point. I couldn't resist seeing the surrounding vistas from the highest point. Ten minutes later, I was looking out over the island with clear and near-unobstructed sea views in all directions — simply magical.

Visiting the Moai nursery to see where they originated was a fascinating experience. We can now also say we'd climbed to the top of a volcano on the world's remotest landmass. Brilliant!

Just a short distance from the nursery and well within sight of the volcano's rim was the sight of an ahu (platform) with no less than fifteen Moai standing on it. Those were just some of the Moai that had been re-erected in recent history. One of those standing Moai had its topknot, or headpiece, sitting on top of it. Many of the Moai had that red lava rock headpiece in place. It was thought to reflect the hairstyle of the men or deities the Moai represented.

Moving and erecting a several-ton Moai statue carved from the rock must have been a feat of incredible engineering, given it all took place thousands of years ago. How they managed to get that separate topknot piece of hefty rock subsequently balanced on top was even more of a mystery.

Between all the bumping around in the four-by-four across rough terrain and the climbing of the steep volcano, we were now exhausted. Sandy has tolerated it all exceptionally well, given the circumstances. We could never be more than 15 km (9 miles) from Hanga Roa regardless of where we were on the island, so a quick ride back into town to grab lunch and, perhaps, a nap was an excellent idea. That was precisely what we did.

I swung by the town's ATM to withdraw some local currency. That should have saved us some money since the rate to the US dollar offered by local businesses was relatively poor compared to the bank's rate. I withdrew CLP100,000 (€137). That would be handy for the two days we planned to spend in Santiago if we didn't spend it all on Easter Island first.

All the shops were closed for the afternoon. I presumed that was to allow everyone to take in their midday siesta[3]. We did manage to find

---

[3] A siesta isn't a widespread tradition on Easter Island, although we didn't know this then.

one small supermarket cum convenience store from which to buy a few bread rolls, some eggs, and a tub of margarine. We converted these into boiled egg sandwiches for our lunch at the house.

Sandy then went off for her afternoon nap, and I did my best to sit at the laptop in the dining room to catch up on my journal updates that I felt were starting to get a bit too far behind. I did that for as long as I could, but those bloody dogs kept at it nonstop again until I could no longer tolerate it. They were steadily driving me to distraction to the point that I couldn't concentrate any more. That was the last straw.

I whipped out the guidebook, located all the places to stay on the opposite side of town, and set off in the Jeep to see if they had any rooms. It was clear that we were to get no real sleep while staying at this location, and it was hard to appreciate any place when we were sleep-deprived.

I followed the guidebook's map as best I could. However, not only did the guidebook's map not accurately reflect the roads on the other side of town (nor indeed this side of town), but the road I was looking for wasn't on the map at all.

After stopping to ask for directions a few times, I finally found the place I was looking for and was extremely pleased to discover the owner spoke perfect English.

At US $50 (€38.46) per night, it was slightly more expensive for the same room quality but a much quieter environment. The woman there also gave me a wealth of first-class information about the island and its hidden treasures.

The new pension owner also confirmed what we already knew about the restaurant where we ate last night: It was one of the worst on the island. As a bonus, several important Moai were down by the shore, just a few minutes on foot. The best Easter Island sunset could be seen from there.

The additional cost would be more than worth it in the long run for the added comfort of having someone around with whom we could effectively communicate. She even wrote me a note in Spanish to give to our current pension owner, explaining that we needed to check out tomorrow morning.

I drove back to our pension and excitedly told Sandy about this new place I'd found with an accommodating proprietor. Since it was late in the day, we'd still have to remain here in this noisy hellhole for tonight, but at least we had better digs to look forward to from tomorrow.

The sun still hadn't set, so we went back out to explore more. We went, in fact, to that sunset location, as the new pension owner advised. It was, indeed, quite a picturesque setting for sunset photography.

We also spent some time near the local beach, where the now-fading sunset presented some scenic views. We ended up eating at one of the restaurants recommended by the guidebook. It was a nice enough meal, if a little sparse and basic, but we received an interesting look from the water after we paid the bill. It hit us afterwards that we had miscalculated the tip and left only about three per cent instead of the customary ten per cent.

Back at the hostel, the owner was not around, but a man I presumed to be her husband was. Like the proprietor, he also spoke no English. I handed him the Spanish-written note from the new pension owner. He read it aloud, smiled, and said no problem. I guessed that meant we were off the hook. I was so glad we hadn't yet paid for the room.

Day 391: Monday, 4th April, 2005, Hanga Roa

We knew that we were in for a noisy night again last night. From that perspective, we weren't proved wrong. Some earplugs from our complimentary in-flight travel kit helped ease the pain a little, but it was another restless night.

When it came time to check out, the man of the house was on duty again. He gave us a slip of paper with our bill total written on it. Still groggy from having woken up, I did my best to figure out what the large number printed on the receipt represented but couldn't quite get my head around it. Sandy and I discussed it and did our best to interpret it based on the exchange rate.

The problem was that we weren't too sure which exchange rate they had used. We had expected to be better off paying in Pesos since everybody except for the bank used a poor exchange rate. After a bit of head-scratching, the penny dropped. They used the bank's exchange rate to charge us in Pesos for the room based on the dollar amount we had been initially told. Essentially, that eliminated any advantage we might have gained by paying in Pesos. The difference was just a few dollars, and I didn't want to make a fuss since those people earned their livelihoods from people like us anyway. I paid the man, and we were on our way.

Just a short five-minute ride through town later, we were unpacking again in our new digs. Tomorrow, I expected to be writing about how much better off we would or wouldn't have been for staying in a more expensive place. We shall see.

Kai, the guy I met and spoke with briefly yesterday when I came over to check this new place out, was sitting there relaxing. We enjoyed exchanging a few more Easter Island travel anecdotes with him. As we were unloading the Jeep and making ourselves at home, a truck arrived and unloaded one of several gas cylinders it was transporting. The owner's mother was a charming motherly figure who took a great interest in whether all the guests were eating well. She was pottering about but seemed in a pickle regarding the gas delivery.

That gas delivery man needed to be paid, but the owner wasn't around. After a bit of a discussion amongst us all, Kai handed over about US $60 of his own money. The idea was that he and the owner would settle eventually. That one-and-a-half-metre tall gas bottle would serve the pension's kitchen, six guest rooms, and their combined heating and cooking needs for about a month.

We were keen to return to the road to explore the island further. Kai came with us again for the ride. We headed north up to the Northern coastline to see what was known as *the naval of the world*. A near-perfectly spherical geode or stone ball had been ejected from one of the volcanoes and landed near the shoreline. We found the location, which yet another fallen Moai marked, but we had to search around a bit for the sphere since there weren't any signs. We eventually found the slightly flattened, one-metre diameter stone ball with four smaller stone balls surrounding it and further encircled by a one-metre tall, artificial lava rock wall.

It wasn't especially awe-inspiring, and I doubted we would have made the journey up to the island's north end just to see it, but it was interesting nevertheless.

Kai was particularly keen to visit the volcano nursery we visited yesterday, so we headed in that direction to drop him off whilst we went elsewhere. We travelled much slower over the dirt track across the top of the island and made it as far as the fifteen upstanding Moai, where we dropped him off to wander around on his own for a while.

In the meantime, a hilly peak occupied the island's northeast corner. Our map showed a track leading up and around to the top. I wanted to drive up there to look at the summit's views, so we agreed to meet Kai back at the volcano when we were done.

We had to pass through what looked like a farm on the foothills of the gentle, sloping, grassy peak. The dirt track that led up and around that huge mound was very uneven and lumpy. Sandy did not enjoy the ride. We were travelling slower than we could have walked at times. Besides a small cluster of trees we passed, the hills were covered in nothing more than tufts of grass. There must have been a couple dozen cows meandering around the hillsides, and we saw plenty of hawks flying about.

It took us well over half an hour to reach the top of the hill. The views were stunning, but we also wanted to find the Moai and petroglyphs that our map indicated were near the top. Petroglyphs were a strange and yet un-deciphered language of pictograms, unlike the hieroglyphs of ancient Egypt. Examples were scattered around the island at various locations. We'd seen souvenirs depicting them but had not seen any for ourselves.

We found a couple of toppled Moai but never did find the petroglyphs. We kept climbing and climbing. Each time we reached the apex of the next hill, more hills appeared in the distance, so we decided to give up on the petroglyphs and turned around instead. The road back down was no less bumpy. I wasn't in Sandy's good books for a while.

Back at the volcano, we met up with Kai and another traveller who had arrived by bike. He was toting one of the town's many stray dogs. He had fed the dog a few morsels of his breakfast, and that new companion followed him on his bike the 13 km (8 miles) to the volcano. Two other dogs had also followed him yesterday.

Near the middle of the island was another row of standing Moai. We wanted to investigate those, so we headed back south again. On the way there, we passed a Japanese cyclist we'd already seen a couple of times. She was having a terrible time pushing her bike uphill and into the wind. Had we had the room, we would have offered her a lift in the Jeep.

Our flat and even paved road eventually gave way to another rough and bumpy dirt track as we headed inland. Fortunately, it wasn't a very long road. It terminated at our row of upstanding Moai.

It didn't matter how many strange statues I saw; they remained enigmatic. There was just something about them that was captivating.

The volcanic geology of Easter Island had littered it with various caves. Those were also highlighted on our map, although extremely difficult to locate. One was nearby, so we detoured just a bit to find it.

The natural caves were formed by lava flows from the various volcanoes gradually cooling. This one was large enough to have been used hundreds, if not thousands, of years ago by the then-inhabitants of the island. They were used to hide the townsfolk from marauding invaders. The false walls they erected to seal off the cave entrances to keep their presence hidden could still be seen, although they had partially been dismantled — perhaps by the marauding invaders.

Our last island destination for the day was to be back up on the North Coast again. A pristine white sand beach in a semi-circular cove was the site of yet another group of standing Moai, most of which still had their topknots. That was a very popular place, and the locals flocked there every Sunday morning after Sunday mass on a free bus service.

When we arrived, the beach was very sparsely populated. The fluffy, white sand and warm, clear waters were so inviting under the heat of the afternoon sun that I just had to take a dip, so I stripped to my undies and dived right in — absolute bliss.

The cove was Punctuated with tall palm trees, and some food stalls sold local snacks and cold beers. The whole setting was idyllic and much nicer than anything we saw on Tahiti.

After half an hour of lazing around in the shallows, I did my best to dry off under the sun, and we slowly made our way back to Hanga Roa, about a twenty-minute drive South to the island's opposite end.

Once we arrived home, I had to get the owner to figure out why I wasn't getting any hot water, but he sorted it out in the end, and I enjoyed a blissful hot shower.

Sandy went for her afternoon nap whilst Kai and I sat at the laptop, looking through some of our travel photos. Kai was a freelance writer. He suggested I consider getting some of my travelogues published (and here we are 20 years later).

Although there was some cloud cover by now, we strolled down to the shore nearby to see if we could take in the sunset. It was too late. By the time we arrived, the sun had dipped below the horizon. We did see something very odd, however. What appeared to be a light aircraft approached the island and landed at the airport. That was curious since the nearest landmass is Chile, several thousand kilometres away. Where could such a small aircraft have come from? We later learned it was a small, private jet flying a dozen passengers from South America.

After all the driving and bumpy roads I had subjected Sandy to today, she was now in the mood to be fed, fed well and without reservation or complaint about the bill. With those marching orders, we searched for one of the better restaurants in town.

We tried the French restaurant our new pension owner told me about yesterday. It was a very chic restaurant with prices to match. I did my best to subdue my misgivings about the cost of the meal, although I must admit that I did not do so very successfully. We were both hungry. I worried we'd have to pay royally for a meagre meal that *looked* fantastic. We both ordered the filet mignon. It was probably the best that we had ever eaten — absolutely delicious. That quite took me by surprise. I could easily see us eating there again tomorrow — even if it cost us another CLP29,000 (€40).

Instead of returning home immediately, we wanted to walk off dinner. I had the bright idea of driving into the middle of the island and away from Hanga Roa's light pollution. We could then enjoy the brilliant show of the Milky Way there in the middle of the ocean. The stars had been out in force overhead. Tonight, however, a thin yet very persistent layer of cloud was steadily developing. That obscured most of the night sky. We may try again tomorrow night.

Day 392: Tuesday, 5th April, 2005, Hanga Roa

Our new location on the other side of the town proved sufficiently far enough away from the howling dogs closer to the airport. It allowed us a peacefully quiet night. Any advantage afforded me by that was swiftly compensated for, however, when I started to develop a bit of an upset stomach halfway through the night. I was up and down to the toilet constantly from then on. I'd have to guess that whatever the bug I picked up, it must have come from the expensive French restaurant last night, although there was no way to be sure.

By the time we awoke this morning, I was exhausted from the lack of sleep and groggy from the ill effects of my tummy bug. My muscles were aching all over, my skin felt hyper-sensitive, and I had a bit of a headache.

We carried with us an exhaustive supply of different medications. Fortunately, we have not needed to plunder it so far. I decided to raid it this morning to find something to rapidly shut down my digestive system. Within 10 minutes of taking a small pill, I felt much better.

Kai was suffering from the same and was grateful for the instant relief he also benefitted from one of those tablets we gave him. We still felt drained and sluggish for the rest of the day.

There were no toilets on the island outside of Hanga Roa, so driving around in a four-by-four on bumpy roads would not be fun while trying to tackle traveller's diarrhoea. Even if it did mean keeping the bug in the system for a bit longer, shutting down the digestive system as a whole was sometimes the best alternative. I'd probably pop another one of those pills tomorrow for the flight to Santiago.

All three of us set out in the Jeep again this morning. Our primary destination was the Rano Kau Volcano, past the airport in the far Southwest tip of the island. That was where the majority of the island's petroglyphs could be found. It was also the location of the dwellings from the Birdman cult era.

We took the Jeep up and around the rough road towards the crater's rim. There was a small car park with several signs in Spanish, so we stopped there and started to explore the area on foot.

The winding path up towards the top of the volcano rim was blustery. We practically leant into the wind at points just to stay on our feet. The view down into the volcano's crater alone was worth the effort to make it up there.

A lake or swamp occupied the crater's centre, several hundred metres below us. A species of grass growing down in the centre was only found in one other location on the earth — Lake Titicaca in Peru. That was one of a couple of clues on the island that suggest a possible Peruvian influence from hundreds or even thousands of years ago. We were to visit the other clue later in the day.

After enjoying the view, Sandy relaxed in the Jeep while Kai and I explored more on foot. We followed a trail around the tip of the rim for several hundred metres until we caught sight of a small building. It was the building where we had to pay our park entrance fees, so Kai walked on while I backtracked to collect Sandy and the Jeep.

The park entrance fees were CLP5,000 (€6.85) or US $5.50 (€4.23) per person, depending on our preferred currency. It covered this and all the other sites around the island. Strangely, this remote location was the only place on the island where a park entrance fee could be made. We could explore the entire island except for this little enclave without paying the park fees if we so desired. Since we'd made it this far and it wasn't a high price to explore the whole island, we handed over our last CLP10,000 (€13,70) note and checked out the old dwellings and petroglyphs.

The Birdman cult ruins were strange enough, and the petroglyphs were fascinating, but I was more impressed with the views into the Rano Kau volcano's crater and out over the cliffs to the nearby small islands than anything else.

We next wanted to visit the site by the coast at the far end of the extended runway. Once again, our less-than-perfect maps were of little use to us. Our progress was further hampered by the worse-than-useless road signs dotted around the place. Not only were they difficult to understand when they could be found, but one was also pointing in the wrong direction altogether. It took some looking around, but we eventually found the ahu with its toppled Moai down by the coast.

There were dozens of toppled Moai all around the island. The one we were interested in was no more impressive than the others, but the ahu on which they formerly stood was significant. The irregularly shaped rocks that form the ahu base were cut and joined with incredible precision and with no gaps between the joins — just like the rock walls of Machu Picchu in Peru. That was the second of the island's two clues hinting at a potential Peruvian influence from centuries ago.

In standing to admire that last ahu site, we had essentially completed our tour of Easter Island, having taken in just about all the major sites. We now headed back into town to pick up some bread and perhaps do some souvenir hunting. We were largely thwarted in the latter because it was siesta time again, and almost everywhere was closed. We did find one small supermarket that was open. Sandy picked out some bread rolls as well as a few postcards. We also located one of the town's Internet cafés, which was still open, so we spent thirty minutes catching up on e-mail chores.

We struck out on the souvenir hunting. A few small places were open, but the posted prices made it seem like we weren't getting the bargain we hoped for. Reluctantly, we decided to head for the artisan's market tomorrow morning before catching our Chile-bound flight. We were now looking forward to a nap and resting back at the pension.

In addition to the small jet that landed the other day, another non-scheduled flight had arrived. A chartered passenger airliner and some two hundred passengers landed. They were travelling en mass on a year-long round-the-world expedition. At the sunset point near our accommodation that evening, there was to be an open-air music and dance performance put on for their benefit. We strolled down there to have a look for ourselves. What we saw turned out to be one of the highlights of our entire Easter Island stay.

The area surrounding the standing Moai by that part of the coast formed a natural amphitheatre. A hundred or more people sat on the grass in a semi-circle around a cordoned-off section where the artists were to perform their songs and dances.

As dusk transitioned to night, flame touches were lit all around the arena. The whole atmosphere was magical, with the bright stars overhead and the gentle sea breeze. I felt something otherworldly about the atmosphere. As a bonus, many of the town's market traders had set up their wares on tables or sheets in a nearby field. Everything was arranged to benefit the recently arrived charter flight and its passengers.

Like us, other visitors and islanders also wandered around enjoying the evening. I particularly enjoyed walking around the market stalls and trying to haggle with the traders to buy a few souvenirs. It took me right back to Victoria Falls in Zimbabwe.

Sandy and I picked up some beautiful keepsakes to take away with us. We spent about US $100 (€76.92) on a few pieces of carved curios. That was just the sort of circumstance that made me regret that we were budget travellers. I could quite easily have spent much more on souvenirs, but we were constricted by budget, weight, and bulk allowances — a pity.

The cultural display of song and dance lasted three-quarters of an hour. The amplified music was superb. We enjoyed watching the performers in their scant ceremonial clothing and mud-decorated skin. They wielded various ceremonial instruments of warfare and danced energetically around the arena. We had not anticipated the opportunity to see such a unique display of cultural excellence. I couldn't think of a better way to complete our stay on that remote island. It was an unexpected yet extremely pleasant culmination of a successful Easter Island trip.

Since the souvenir purchases that evening represented the last of the expenditure there on Easter Island, let me reflect a bit on how much passing through had cost us. As always, I'll ignore the cost of the flights since they were all wrapped up in the total round-the-world flight package. Altogether, we spent precisely €499 during our four-day visit to Rapa Nui, the local name for Easter Island. I had budgeted €120 per day for the two of us, so we were just €19 over budget. Had we not spent more on our second choice of accommodation, not eaten at the very expensive (relatively speaking) restaurants, not purchased lots of souvenirs or not forked out on a four-by-four Jeep for the duration, we could quite easily have reduced this amount considerably. But that wasn't the point. We were there to experience Easter Island and to enjoy ourselves. That was precisely what we did — no regrets.

CHILE

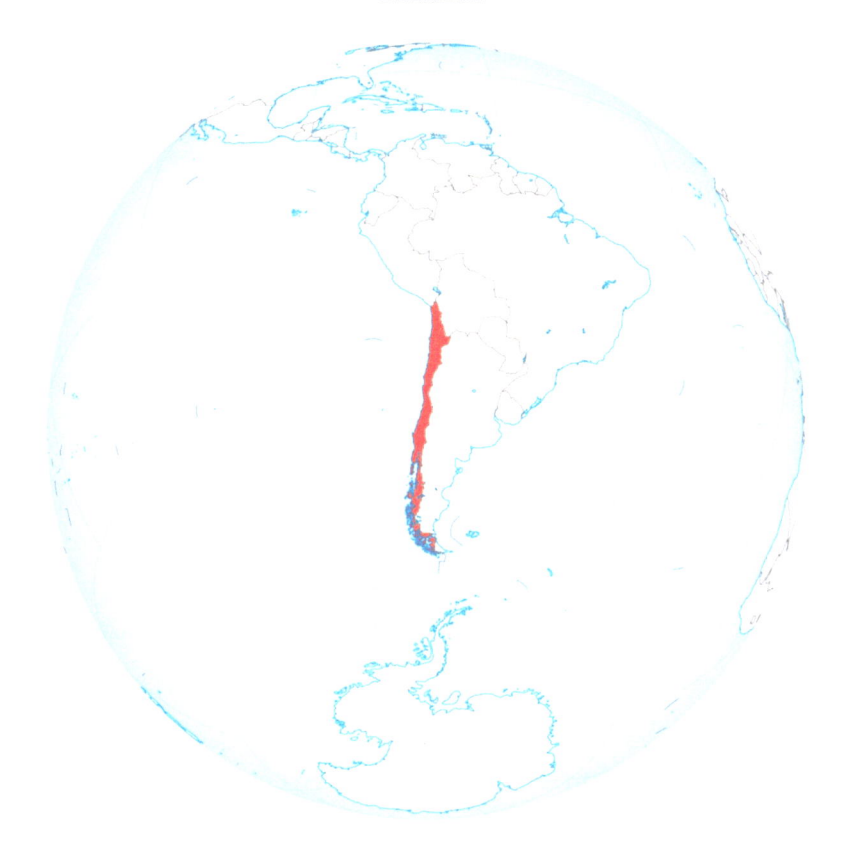

Day 393: Wednesday, 6th April, 2005, Santiago

I didn't feel like breakfast much this morning, but Sandy threw together some sandwiches for herself. What looked like a lovely breakfast was laid on in the main house this morning. However, neither of us was too impressed with the kitchen's hygiene, so we weren't particularly eager to eat there anyway.

I paid the outstanding US $100 (€76.92) bill for our two nights of accommodation, and we said our goodbyes to the staff and Kai, whom the owner's mother rather unceremoniously shook out of bed so that he could *say goodbye* to his *friends*. It was always refreshing to share a few days with another traveller. We enjoyed Kai's company tremendously, as we had done with previous people with whom we temporarily shared the travelling experience. These off-chance encounters with other travellers were all part of the experience, and we felt richer after meeting them.

Per the Jeep rental woman's instructions, we left the vehicle at the airport with the keys in the ignition. That rough and ready four-by-four served us well for the past four days.

Many of the people at the small terminal building were those we'd bumped into around the island and in town over the past few days. We enjoyed exchanging a few anecdotes of our time on the island with each other.

The queue of passengers was being very slowly checked in. The wait in line would have been less irritating if it hadn't been for the German package tourists immediately behind me, who were doing their utmost to move ahead through the line faster than it was naturally moving. It seemed to take forever for the line to whittle down to the last remaining passengers. Despite that, the plane miraculously managed to take off on schedule.

Given that the flight was almost exclusively over the open ocean, there wasn't much I could comment on regarding the journey. What was interesting, nevertheless, was the fact that we passed near the real Robinson Crusoe Island off the coast of Chile, the Isla Robinson Crusoe, part of the Juan Fernández Archipelago. That's near in relative terms. Our flight path didn't bring us closer than around 370 km (230 miles) to the island.

We started our descent just as we approached the mainland, about 140 Km (75 miles) from Santiago. By then, the sun was very low in the sky. The mountain ranges of the Andes looked particularly spectacular, with a light mist hanging in the air that allowed the low sun to cast some eerie shadows between the peaks and valleys.

Once again, we found ourselves arriving in a new place, indeed a new and very different region of the world, completely blind. That is, we didn't know where we would stay or how we would even get out of the airport once we collected our bags. Worse still, neither of us spoke any Spanish.

I must admit to being somewhat apprehensive about what Chile had to throw at us. It was, after all, our first real foray into South America (excluding, for the moment, Easter Island). South America was the one region of the world anywhere on our itinerary I confess to knowing the least about.

South America had never really been high on my priorities as a travel destination. We were never going to spend much time on that continent, so I hadn't devoted much time and energy to researching it. Admittedly, we originally planned to spend time in Peru exploring Machu Picchu, but that was one of the destinations we cut from the itinerary once we learned of Sandy's pregnancy. The closer a country was to the end of the itinerary, the less time I had spent researching it. Most of my time had been spent investigating the regions of the world earlier on in the itinerary.

For every other country we'd visited, I've been able to tell Sandy, for example, all about what to expect. In so doing, I could exude a certain degree of confidence towards her. That had helped put any fears or apprehensions she might have had to rest in the past. I'd been the driving force behind this endeavour, with Sandy following me metaphorically. I'd tried to explain what was to come and what to expect as we moved from one country to the next. Chile, or South America as a whole, was the first destination for which I couldn't do that. The exception was the Galapagos Islands. That was one location that I knew more about because of my enthusiasm for the natural world and the links to Charles Darwin and his 1831-1836 voyage on the HMS Beagle. For now, the Galapagos Islands were a long way away.

For all my apprehensions about South America, I'd have to confess I'd been entirely impressed with Chile. All the usual formalities at the airport went very smoothly. Even the immigration officer seemed like a nice man. All he wanted to know was where we had just flown in from.

As we walked towards the baggage belt, my attention was caught by a charming young lady standing at a small booth with a backlit display full of hotel listings. I swallowed my instinct to be wary about that sort of touting and went to talk with her. Since we were still waiting for our bags to arrive, it didn't seem like any harm. She was lovely. She told me about places to stay within our budget range — as cheap as possible.

My traveller's instincts to be wary and sceptical were starting to break down. Ultimately, what sold me was that one of the places she represented was on the same street but just a couple of doors away, as the one place we intended to try out first from our guidebook listing. She called them to ensure they had a room and then wrote a receipt for me. I told her that I would need to see the room before paying any money, but that wasn't a problem since the idea was for me to pay the hotel directly anyway. I figured I could at least show up, check it out, and walk up the street to our first choice anyway if it was no good.

She pointed out the various options for getting into town. They all matched exactly what our guidebook told us, so her stock went up a bit more with that, too.

There wasn't a metro station at the airport. The cheapest way to get into town was by bus, then metro, and then on foot. We didn't fancy the idea of that much stress with it getting very dark. Just across the other side of the baggage belt were another couple of booths where we could buy our way onto one of several regularly departing minibuses. They would drop us and our luggage off at the hotel's door. I showed them the little brochure of the hotel I'd just received. We bought a couple of return trip vouchers for US $10 (€7.69) each.

I explained to the shuttle booth attendant that we weren't sure which hotel we would stay at since we planned to check them out first. That wasn't a problem. I just had to call to let them know once we were settled, and they would collect us from there when it was time to use the return portion of the voucher.

So far, then, everything had gone smoothly. All the usual new destination arrival hassles had been lifted from our tired shoulders. We collected our bags and walked straight through customs. Immediately behind the sliding glass doors was the uniformed shuttle bus driver. He took our trolley and helpfully loaded all our bags into the waiting minibus outside.

As luck would have it, we were the last of half a dozen or more passengers to be collected in this shuttle and thus departed immediately. We hadn't been anywhere yet where we'd been so well looked after right from the get-go (except those places where we'd met friends or relatives). So far, South America had welcomed us warmly.

The drive into town was about half an hour. What immediately struck me was the well-developed country infrastructure around me. I had half-imagined South America to be third-world, with developing facilities in general. Santiago, at least, had a well-developed airport and road system with a lot of advertising for consumer goods, much like I might have expected from Europe or North America.

During the brief drive, I became aware that I was no longer holding onto any apprehension or misgivings. I felt at ease. I was only concerned about the driver's slightly heavy right foot as he zipped through the city traffic, trying to one-up all the other road users. Judging by the flow of traffic and the general manners of all the other motorised vehicles on the road, that was the norm there. As cars and buses were busy cutting each other up, I was reminded of how things were in Cairo, although it was considerably worse there.

Santiago was a sprawling metropolis, much like any other large city. From what we could see through the fading sunlight, it lacked the cluster of skyscrapers many cities touted, but it was still a very active and lively metropolis. Some parts that we drove through were reminiscent of Delhi and Cairo. Sometimes, it felt like we could have been moving through London or Paris. The five-ball juggler entertaining traffic for small change at a red traffic light was amusing.

Just one other passenger was dropped off before we reached our hotel. We were staying in a quaint part of the city with cobblestone streets and architectural splendours that beckoned to be visited during the daylight hours of tomorrow.

Our driver politely offloaded our bags and was away. Rather than take the luggage straight into the hotel, I had Sandy sit with it all outside while I checked the accommodate. If it didn't look good, we could walk the few metres across to the opposite side of the narrow and winding street to check out other places, including a couple listed in our guidebook.

One of the pleasant young ladies at the reception desk spoke some English. Rather than telling her I had a receipt from the airport, I thought I'd ask her how much a double room would be. To my surprise, it was the same price we were given at the airport. I asked her if I could see the room. After persuading her that my wife was pregnant and unable to climb many stairs, she had one of the hotel maids show us a room just around the corner on the ground floor.

The room was very spacious, had good security, and had its own bathroom. As with all the buildings in that part of town, our hotel was older but had a lot of character. Breakfast was included in the US $34 (€26.15) rate room, and there was a kitchen and free Internet use. What more could we want?

I told the receptionist I was happy with the room and that I was going outside to collect my wife and our baggage. Once outside, I told Sandy to stay put while I quickly dashed over to the other side of the street to check out the other place. However, the first thing that struck me was a flight of stairs leading up to the reception area on the first floor. That was all I needed to see to convince me. I collected Sandy, and we checked into our ground-floor room from where I had emerged moments earlier.

As Sandy was comfortable in our new temporary home, I wasted no time checking the Internet. That turned out to be a pretty respectable speed. Unfortunately, some bad news was awaiting me from Holland.

Our campervan had failed its APK, the mandatory annual safety check-up (which is referred to as the MOT in the UK). I was now facing more bills to fix the battery and brakes. Would that problem ever go away? Our guardian angel in Holland, Dinie, was handling things for us but still needed my input on how to proceed. I spent a few minutes writing her back. Hopefully, we could sort everything out before we got to the Galapagos Islands, where I was sure Internet access would be extremely limited.

The streets of Santiago were alive. Thousands of pedestrians were going about their business. I always felt a sense of safety and security in a bustling town or city, so we ventured out to explore. Although we could use US dollars for many things in Chile, we still needed some local currency. It took just a few minutes to locate a nearby ATM and withdraw CLP70,000 (€95,89) to keep us going for the next two days.

A main road just a short walk from our hotel building marked a clear division between two parts of the city. We were in what appeared to be an older sector of town with narrow, winding, cobblestone streets. It was replete with elegant architecture that housed mostly hotels. The city took on a more modern feel on the other side of the bustling road. There were considerably more pedestrians buzzing around, as well as dozens of restaurants and other food outlets.

We found a petite eatery in the restaurant district. I did my level best, using little more than primitive sign and body language, to try to place an order for our evening meal. Pictures of food on a backlit sign above the counter helped. I could point to things as we went through the ordering process. It was more like a cafeteria than a formal restaurant. I took the fact it was packed with locals to be a good sign. The hard-working wait staff were generously tolerant of me (and my one- to two-word Spanish sentences) and managed to bring out exactly what we thought we were ordering in the end.

In Thailand, we bought several bottles of coconut oil used for massaging. We purchased and sent some bottles home for ourselves but kept one with us in our backpacks. Since Sandy was pregnant, she had been using it on her stomach. It helped to keep her skin dry, and she had read somewhere that it could help prevent or reduce the effect of stretch marks. We thought we left our coconut oil bottle behind by mistake somewhere recently. We couldn't find it anywhere in our backpacks. Since we were now in a large city with an endless supply of shops, we went to see if we could pick up another bottle.

So it came to pass that we had recently arrived on a new continent and were exploring a major city looking for coconut oil to rub on my wife's tummy, even though we had no idea what to ask for in the local language or how to describe it tactfully using sign language.

We made several attempts to ask for it at pharmacies. We even tried a supermarket. Each time, the language barrier proved insurmountable for something that complex. We eventually had to abandon the quest. We thought the next thing we should look for might have been an English-Spanish phrasebook instead.

Back at the hotel, I had the receptionist call the shuttle bus company to confirm our airport transfer pickup for the day after tomorrow. That she did without hesitation or reservation and even with a smile. Everything was now settled. We had our place to stay right in the thick of things, some local currency in our pocket, and our onward transportation all sorted. We could now devote the entire day tomorrow to sleeping in and enjoying what Santiago offered.

Day 394: Thursday, 7th April, 2005, Santiago

It must have been the jetlag that caused us both to be so restless last night. We couldn't sleep for several hours after trying to put our heads down. We ended up sitting up into the wee hours watching a Sylvester Stallone B movie.

Over the past few weeks, we'd made tremendous progress around the planet in an Easterly direction. We'd flown from New Zealand to Tahiti to Easter Island to South America in less than a week. Each of those displacements had been a four or five-hour flight. We'd lost a couple of hours to the time zone fairy each time. The resulting jetlag we now suffered was an unfortunate by-product of that Easterly direction of travel around the globe. If we were ever to repeat the exercise, I'd perhaps choose for us to travel in the opposite direction instead.

Travel days were generally very tiring. After spending an exhausting day on the move, we typically wanted the day to be longer than usual and not shorter. We both suffered from the effects of jetlag, but Sandy eventually went to sleep before me. I never got a significant stretch of sleep all through the night.

At one point, I realised my nose was blocked, and I was worried that the fatigue plaguing my body was lowering my natural defences. I ran the risk of a common cold or something sneaking in. As luck would have it, I finally awoke this morning feeling surprisingly absent of any illness. My nose was no longer blocked, although I still felt groggy and stiff.

We thought we'd try the complimentary breakfast in the dining room that morning. Much like any hotel, this one had a dedicated dining room, so we slipped in to sit at one of the nicely laid-out breakfast tables.

A couple of other people were sitting there finishing their tea or coffee, but there were no wait staff as far as we could see. Eventually, one of the maids came in and put a pot of hot water on the table. Several minutes later, another maid came in and handed us each a glass of overly sweet juice. A third maid came in a while later and placed some butter on the table. It went on like that for the next half an hour, with tiny bits of our breakfast being brought in piecemeal. I wasn't going to put up with the usual slice of bread, butter, jam and tea or coffee that morning, so I went to the reception desk and asked the one passable English-speaking woman I knew would be there if I could get some eggs with my breakfast.

She informed me their complimentary breakfast didn't typically include eggs but that it wouldn't be a problem and that I should ask the maid. She told me what the correct Spanish phrase was for ordering eggs. However, my brain could barely manage coherent motor function within my first waking hour of the day, let alone that sort of linguistic complexity. I had her write it down for me.

I showed this to the maid back in the dining room, and she nodded. Then, she disappeared into the kitchen. Yet another new maid soon returned and asked me something in Spanish. I could only assume she asked how I wanted my eggs cooked, so I tried to convey the message that I wanted them boiled. I pointed to the hot pot of water on the table as I tried to explain, but she then went away and came back with a teabag so that clearly didn't work for me.

I was unsure if she understood the resignation in my sunken nod to her as she put the teabag down and disappeared again. I did my best to prevent my head from falling forward into my breakfast with a thud. Sandy quietly chuckled. I didn't know how many maids they had there, but another new face soon came out of the kitchen with a skillet of scrambled eggs. It was clear the scrambled eggs were about as close to getting what I wanted without putting in considerably more effort, so I made do with them. At least we had something to eat.

We'd been accumulating souvenirs again since I picked up that boomerang in Australia. Add that to the curios from New Zealand and Easter Island, as well as a few guidebooks and other bits and pieces we carried around but no longer needed, and our backpacks were starting to feel heavy again. We'd been stuffing more and more things into the originally near-empty box that contained just the boomerang. That was now a rather heavy third piece of carry-on luggage, and it is high time we sent it home.

We sought the main post office in the middle of the city centre that morning. It was a rather elegant building that oozed character — on the outside, at least. On the inside, there was a spacious atrium in the middle with all the usual post-office-type departments around the inside, slowly tending to queues of people and their postal needs. One queue was not just very long; it doubled back and forth several times. That queue looked like it would take an eternity to make it through. I found a smaller queue of people lining up in front of what looked like an information booth. I tacked onto that one, hoping the woman slowly handling those customers might speak at least a little English.

Some of the customers in the line were frustrated by the slow progress. Overall, however, they seemed to take it largely in good spirits and were generally smiling as they complained amongst themselves.

It was a while before I got to the front. The woman turned out to not speak any English. Curiously, she seemed to understand what I wanted when I pointed to my parcel and tried to tell her in my shamelessly inadequate Spanish that I wanted to send it to England. I tried to get her to tell me how much it would cost to send, but they were having problems with the computer. I had to wait for several more people around me to be served before she could do so.

I needed to repack the contents into a larger box to accommodate the gold panning bowl we'd been toting since New Zealand. The only boxes they had were either too big or too small. We gave up on the re-packaging and decided to send the parcel as it was, sans bowl.

I tried to hand it over after filling out the requisite forms. She handed it back to me with the sort of pitying look that said something like, 'Look at this poor sap, he doesn't understand.' She mumbled something to me in Spanish. There was a problem with the package, but it wasn't evident what that problem was. Did she need the package contents to first customs-inspected, perhaps? My most pathetic dear-in-the-headlights stare must have solicited pity from the surrounding customers as they all started to mumble to each other. One of them wrote a few words down on a piece of paper for me. I looked at her and the words written on the piece of paper. Everyone then started to point at the door leading out to the street. They seemed to be egging me on to leave the building as if to say, 'Go on lad, that's right, you can do it.'

So, with my package under my arm and this piece of paper in my hand, off we wandered out into the street, not that we had any idea where we were going or what our purpose was. We walked around a bit and stopped several people whilst pointing at the note, but nobody seemed to understand.

I distinctly got the impression that some of them were internally mocking this poor foreign idiot, clutching a strange package and who was aimlessly wandering around the streets of Santiago, not knowing where he was going or why. I decided to head back to the post office. I noticed a guy standing outside selling wrapping and packaging materials. I showed him the note, and he instantly seemed to understand. He handed me a large, folded sheet of thick, brown wrapping paper and a roll of tape and then held his hand out. I pulled a stack of loose change from my pocket and offered it to him. He helped himself to several larger coins, smiled and appeared to thank me.

Clearly, then, I needed to wrap my already wrapped blue package in brown paper before the post office would accept it. Indeed, we'd encountered this phenomenon before in other countries, notably India and Kenya, so it did seem plausible.

I took the wrapping paper and tape back into the post office, and we wrapped the parcel well and solidly. When I handed it back to the woman at the information booth, she smiled and accepted it this time.

I felt a warm sensation of gratification and accomplishment flow through me for finally solving the riddle and surmounting that minor mountain. Patience and persistence had paid off that time. We were finally able to say goodbye to the package for CLP21,000 (€29). I hoped we'd see it again at some future point.

Our next task for the morning was to find the American Express office. We needed to exchange some of the traveller's checks we'd been carrying since the outset. Our Galapagos Island cruise had to be paid in US dollars cash. I also wanted to ensure we had more than enough readies with us when we arrived in Quito.

Just as soon as we decided to set off and locate the AmEx office, the hindrance of our combined lack of Spanish skills again came to the fore. Subconsciously, I probably thought I'd ask someone the way, but we'd had nearly zero luck finding people who spoke English in Santiago. Trying to stop a random pedestrian was too much of a hit-and-miss affair, so I found a police officer on horseback and asked him for the way to the American Express office.

He seemed to understand and tried to send us off with some simple directions — two blocks up and three over. We followed those directions to the letter but were singularly unsuccessful in finding the AmEx office nearby.

There was a Bureau de Change nearby. I would have bet money on them knowing where it was, so I went in to ask. Nope! One of the customers inside seemed to know where it was. He gave us clear directions to go directly back to where the police officer who sent us there was.

We went back anyway since that was where most of the action was. We eventually ended up stepping into the Bank of Chile after giving up on ever finding the AmEx office.

To cut a very long story short, I could finally cash US $700 (€538.46) of traveller's checks at the bank into US dollars cash for a flat commission of US $18 (€13.85). Added to the US $2,600 (€2,000) cash reserves we already had, I was confident we now had more than enough to cover us for the Galapagos Islands.

I still had several hundred US dollars in traveller's checks if needed. We'd probably cash those in when we got to Florida. By now, we were both irritable from the frustrations of the two tasks that we set ourselves this morning, so we dived straight into the nearest McDonald's for a quick fix. Yes, I know, we were incurable.

If this morning had taught us anything, we had come to this Spanish-speaking region of the world entirely unprepared, linguistically speaking (no pun intended). Something had to be done about that. Our guidebook was seriously lacking in the translation section, so we searched for a bookshop to buy an English-Spanish phrase book.

It may have already been too late to save our remaining dignity, but at least we'd have something to use in emergencies. I knew just a few keywords in Spanish and constantly tried to use them as best I could. The problem was I only knew a few small words. I kept mixing them with Dutch, French and German words, too. When I tried to say 'thank you', 'please', 'excuse me', 'yes', 'no' or whatever else, what came out of my mouth was an incoherent and barely audible dribble that even I did not understand.

Sandy spotted a couple of bookshops in the guidebook, so we headed over there to see what we could find. As luck would have it, they did have just one smallish phrase book that went from English to Spanish, so I took it to the counter to pay for it.

Buying something from a local shop was a different procedure than back home. In Santiago, we took the article we wanted to buy to one counter and exchanged it for a printed ticket. We then had to take that ticket to the cash register for payment. Only then could we collect the now-bagged article we were shopping for.

We'd noticed that two-tier shopping process in several shops we'd entered. It was a similar procedure in the bank when I cashed those traveller's checks earlier. I didn't see the logic or advantage to that approach, but it worked for the Chileans.

It had to be said that every staff member in all the shops we'd been to was extremely helpful and friendly. Many went out of their way to be more helpful than we might reasonably have expected. That all added to our feeling of ease there, even if we were out of our depth in the language department.

Back at the hotel, we had a bit of a rest. I took the opportunity to catch up on some discussions on the Internet about how to get the most out of our impending Galapagos Island trip. The overwhelming consensus amongst seasoned travellers and those in the know was to not book a cruise ahead of time over the Internet. It was even discouraged to book in Quito via the travel agents. The consensus was to book directly with the boat owners upon arrival on the island archipelago. By doing so, the cruises could be had for under half and even a quarter of the advertised prices.

Several people had attested to that, which gave me confidence. I was happy that the approach would work for us, too. Indeed, that buy-it-on-the-spot advice was applicable to just about any travel-related activity across the planet. We learned that through our travels on numerous occasions.

At the recommendation of another traveller, I sent an e-mail to the airline operating the route between Quito and the Galapagos islands in Ecuador. Within the hour, I received a reassuring reply confirming our reservation, although it was one day later than we would have liked. I sent another e-mail to see if we could get on the flight a day earlier to maximise our time on the islands. Hopefully, I will receive a reply to that request by tomorrow morning.

Sandy had another craving for a steak dinner that evening. She had been having more and more of those lately, and I'm not entirely convinced it's unrelated to her pregnancy. Whatever the reason, a decent-quality meal sounded like an excellent idea.

Uncharacteristically, I went through the guidebook listings for local places to eat. I eventually found one whose description met our mutual approval. It was in another part of the city, so we ventured into the metro system.

The brief, three-stop ride cost us each CLP480 (€0,66). At the other end, we had a ten-minute walk. Lunch was the locals' biggest meal of the day, and dinner could often be very late for Chileans. When we arrived at the restaurant, we were too early. They hadn't yet opened for business. We walked around the corner to sip a drink in a nearby café while we perused our new phrase book.

Our restaurant was a jazz joint, but the live-performing musicians didn't set up until at least ten o'clock. We would long since be back in our room by then.

As it turned out, the meal was worth the effort. It was one of the best we'd had for a while. Chilean fare just happened to lean very heavily towards meat and potatoes. That worked out just about perfectly for our own tastes and likes. With tip, the final tally came to CLP17,600 (€24.11) for what probably would have cost us anything up to US $100 (€77) in Florida and probably more still in England or Holland.

We might have considered getting a taxi back to our hotel, but we were now nearly out of local currency. I didn't know if what we had left would cover the fare, so we returned via the way we came instead.

It had been a long day in Santiago. Unfortunately, we would leave the city without even having really seen it. Alas, that was to be the case for South America as a whole. As I kept telling people, the world is just too big.

ECUADOR

Day 395: Friday, 8th April, 2005, Quito

With a little bit of a nudge from Sandy (although I lied about the bit about it being little), I dragged myself out of bed that morning. Since we didn't need to check out until noon and weren't scheduled to be collected to be taken back to the airport until one o'clock, there wasn't any pressing need to get up early. Even though I could have slept well into the afternoon if left unattended, I forced myself into action since I knew I would only be doing myself and my internal body clock a disservice otherwise.

We packed and left our bags locked together behind the reception desk while we went to town to kill some time. We did so by window shopping, grabbing one last bite to eat and looking for new batteries for the underwater strobe. I wanted to arrive in the Galapagos Islands well-prepared for some underwater photography.

While in town, I also withdrew another CLP50,000 (€68,50). I took that to a nearby bank to exchange some of it for a complete collection of Chilean banknotes for my collection. I'd already found one of each coin and had tucked those away safely and soundly.

Our shuttle bus arrived on time but had parked just out of sight from where we sat in the reception area. We discovered that when the driver called the hotel. The receptionist then informed us he was outside waiting for us. Luckily, we were the last passengers to be collected and were whisked immediately off to the airport. Even though we were a full two hours early, the check-in clerk informed us there were no longer any two seats together because so many people had already checked in. Since Sandy was pregnant, she was given the bulkhead seat immediately behind business class. I was assigned a seat in the emergency exit row. Neither of us was complaining.

I kept thinking back to that open-air performance we enjoyed on Easter Island. I remembered how much I enjoyed the music, so I popped into some shops in the departure lounge to see if I could find a CD of traditional Rapa Nui music. I found a couple of different CDs. The second one I tried sounded most like the music from the performance we saw. It may even have been the same performers. I bought the CD for US $17 (€13) and loaded it onto the laptop.

We did our best to whittle away the remainder of the Chilean money. Buying a few snacks was all it took to do so before it was time to board.

After taking my seat, I was met by two other young English travellers, Alyson and Albert. They were two months into their yearlong round-the-world journey and had spent most of their time in South America. We got on immediately and chatted non-stop throughout the five-hour flight about the places we'd each been to and all the things we'd encountered. We agreed to share a taxi into town upon arrival and may spend the day with each other tomorrow. They were lovely people.

Overall, our first impressions of Ecuador had been quite favourable. The airport was modern enough. Although the place had an unmistakable South American feel, it didn't look as third-world as I had anticipated. It was perhaps a little less developed than Chile, but I once again felt my initial apprehensions rapidly evaporating.

Our two new English friends and we, together with a fifth Australian that we got chatting to on the plane, decided to all share a ride into town. That was before getting just a little bit taken for a ride by the eager porters who insisted on carrying our bags ten metres from the glass sliding doors of the arrivals hall to the waiting shuttle bus. Before we knew what was happening, they had already collectively relieved us of US $3 (€2.31). Oh well, at least it was only a dollar each.

Alyson and Albert had already pre-booked a hotel in the same area of town where we were considering staying, so we decided to go straight there and see if it would suit our needs and budget. As it turned out, it was a proper hotel rather than a backpacker's hostel. We liked the idea of a properly serviced room with a bathroom, so we decided to stay there, too.

The receptionist initially wanted US $50 (€38.46), but I bartered him down to US $40 (€30.77). That price included what they described as an American Breakfast. That was a regular South American breakfast, apart from eggs. At least it was something.

A nice touch was the complimentary drink coupon we were each given on arrival at the hotel. The four of us who stayed at the hotel put them to immediate good use with a stiff drink and a snack in the hotel bar. We had a lovely time unwinding over a few drinks. The four of us had decided to spend the day together tomorrow. We planned to visit the nearby Mitad del Mundo. A monument there marks the location of the equator. We may also tour a nearby volcano to peer over the rim, weather permitting.

Day 396: Saturday, 9th April, 2005, Quito

Perhaps it was the alcohol adversely affecting my senses last night, but I didn't notice my mattress was slightly leaning to one side until early this morning. I was suddenly aware of constantly trying to prevent myself from falling onto the floor. Bloody hotels — there's always something.

We went downstairs to the dining room to meet Alyson and Albert for breakfast as per last night's arrangements. I was especially looking forward to getting that American Breakfast. Alas, it was nothing more than a scrambled egg to go with the piece of dry bread and a cup of tea or coffee.

The waitress also brought us all a glass of some fruit punch. I had seen her making it from where we sat at the table. She had put a massive mug of sugar into the solution before dispensing it into glasses, so I asked for a glass without sugar. Unfortunately, with communications being what it was, the only thing I could get out of her was a sense that I would have to make do with this or nothing at all. I wasn't going to take that lying down, especially from a hotel, so I spoke with the English-speaking receptionist about getting a glass of something else without sugar. After a while, a glass of lemonade arrived. When I took a mouthful, I saw half a centimetre of un-dissolved sugar in the bottom of the glass. I wondered whether those things had just happened to me and me alone.

The hotel charged a small fortune per item for laundry, but a launderette was just across the road. Today would be the last opportunity to get the wash done. We desperately needed fresh things to wear, so I took about four kilograms of clothes over there. There was a two-hour turnaround, and all they charged was US $1.56 (€1.20). I couldn't say fairer than that. We'd collect it later when we returned from our day trip to the equator.

It was just a fifteen-minute walk to the bus stop. We stopped at several places along the way to pick up bread rolls and bottled water.

There were many poor people in Quito. Although the roads and pavements are well formed, they were poorly maintained. Litter was strewn everywhere. Still, Quito had a certain charm to it, and the streets were buzzing with people going about their daily business. It was interesting to see the way many of the people of Quito dressed in their traditional clothing and the different types of hats that gave away their cultural backgrounds.

Our clapped-out rattletrap of a bus was full to bursting point not long after we got in, but the forty-five-minute ride out to where the equator lies was not too uncomfortable. We each had to pay US 40¢ (31¢) for the ride.

We found a small complex of craft shops and little museums at the site of the equator, along with a vast monument whose four walls aligned with the four cardinal compass directions. We each had to pay US $1.50 (€1.15) to enter the complex.

Atop the 30 m (98 foot) tall stone monument stood a large globe with a heavy line visible around the equator. A yellow line on the floor marked the exact spot of the equator itself, so naturally, we stood there and took the necessary photos to mark the occasion. It was quite a geographical milestone to stand on the exact location of the equator. It would have been even more impressive had it been true. It turned out that the actual geographical equatorial line was 240 m (790 feet) to the north. When the monument was first constructed from 1979 to 1982, they used measurements from a French scientific expedition in the 18th century. Those weren't as accurate as modern-day methods.

Quito is about 2,850 m (9,350 feet) above sea level. Despite being on the equator (Ecuador is Spanish for equator), it wasn't nearly as warm as I imagined it might have been at the earth's centre. The average temperature in Quito for April was a mere 15^{0}C (58^{0}F). With our warm-weather clothing, we were all feeling the cold.

We were offered a US $6 (€4.62) tour to the top of the nearby volcano and back. With my arms and legs exposed, I worried about the cold temperatures at that higher elevation. We decided to skip it, but Alyson and Albert wanted to go.

We picked up some postcards from the tiny post office inside the complex and had them marked with the equator stamp. We thought it might be fun for someone to receive a postcard from the equator.

Since it was just about lunchtime, we also grabbed a bit from one of the several restaurants inside the complex. The whole place was strangely empty of other tourists. I counted perhaps a dozen people wandering around. By the time we finished lunch, the volcano had disappeared. Huge clouds had lowered over the entire mountain to obscure it completely. After that, Alyson and Albert decided to forgo their hour-and-a-half return trip to the top of the volcano's rim.

According to our guidebook, there was a small museum up the road from this spot where, among other things, we could see a demonstration of the effect of water spin as it falls through a plughole — or lack thereof — at the equator. It was a hundred metres from the main entrance but very poorly signposted. It would have been difficult to find without a deliberate search. Visiting that place was an excellent idea since we learnt a lot about Ecuador's culture and way of life.

We also saw various things relating to Ecuador's historical traditions, some of which were quite disturbing. One was the practice of beheading an enemy, removing their brain and skull, and preserving the resulting shrunken mass to be mounted on the end of a spear. That was done as a deterrent to potential foes. This very unlikely little museum had one such shrunken head on display.

The small gift shop run by a local Ecuadorian family was a lovely treat for the two of us. They were selling various woven mats and other decorative throws. They also had a working loom where they made them right there on the spot. For just US $2 (€1.54) and US $3 (€2.31) per item, we couldn't resist picking up a few things to add to our growing collection of worldly souvenirs.

Our English-speaking guide then took us to another spot in this open-air museum where a line was marked on the ground. That was signposted as the *true equator*. Naturally, we all queried that, having just spent the morning at a nearby megalith of a monument where another equator line was also marked. This was when we learnt about the nature of the accurate equatorial measurements and the unfortunate construction of the Mitad del Mundo monument in the wrong spot. The line on the ground running through this little museum had been verified as the correct location of the equator based on GPS measurements. I had to chuckle at the irony of the whole thing.

We enjoyed ourselves at the little museum and got some nice souvenirs to take home with us. It took us a couple of attempts, but we finally managed to find our way onto the right bus back into Quito. We got out at the airport while Alyson and Albert explored dining options for us all this evening.

I wanted to drop by the airline office tomorrow morning to verify our flights to the Galapagos Islands. When we arrived, we were in for quite a bit of a shock.

I had made the reservation over the Internet the night before last and even received a confirmation e-mail from the airline. After that, I sent another e-mail asking about the price, as well as inquiring if we would be able to fly today if we wanted to. I never received a reply to that second e-mail query. I didn't pay much attention since I already had the confirmation for our flights tomorrow. However, the airline had taken my inquiry about availability for today's flight to be a request to change the booking to today. Not only were we scheduled to fly out today instead of tomorrow, but the flights for tomorrow were now booked solid. It didn't matter how much I tried to explain to the woman behind the counter; she was insistent that she could now do nothing. My repeated protestations eventually drove her to provide me with the phone number of the central reservation office in Quito. She suggested they might be able to help and sent us over to the international terminal, where the information counter might allow us to make the call.

They didn't, as it turned out. However, they suggested we go to the check-in hall to speak to the airline check-in agents. We were lucky enough to track down the supervisor there. Even after several tense minutes of waiting while he and another woman frantically ticked way on their terminals, they could not offer us a confirmed seat. However, they both assured us that if we were here an hour before tomorrow morning's seven-thirty flight, we would stand an excellent chance of getting seats. That was already going to be my original tactic for getting onto the flight, but it was a shame to have lost the confirmed booking.

We jumped into another US $4 (€3.07) taxi outside the arrival hall to return to our hotel. I made sure to have the receptionist arrange our wake-up call and taxi back to the airport for tomorrow morning.

Our laundry was now also ready and neatly folded. I couldn't ever remember paying so little for a load of washing.

As we were resting in our room, Alyson came in with their evening's dining research results. The four of us agreed to splurge that evening, so we planned to travel to Quito's only TGI Friday's. We were all famished and decided to go earlier rather than later. Once again, the local bus transported us across town, this time for just US 25¢ (19¢) each. With a complete disregard for the bill, we gorged ourselves silly on what was a bit of a treat relative to how we'd all been eating over the past few months. With the couple of drinks that I uncharacteristically ordered, the bill for Sandy and me came to about US $43 (€33) — by all accounts, a staggeringly high bill for Ecuador, but none of us was complaining.

Now stuffed to the hilt with good food, we decided a taxi back to the hotel was better than the bus. That just happened to coincide with the recommendation of the guidebook. Travelling around the city after dark was not recommended. Our taxi veered off in the wrong direction for a while, but we reckon that was a miscommunication about our intended destination. Since the fare was just US $3 (€2.31) between the four of us, it didn't seem to make a huge difference, and again, none of us was complaining.

We had a very early start to tomorrow morning, so we bid a sad farewell to Alyson and Albert. I envied them, as they had the bulk of their trip ahead.

GALÁPAGOS ISLANDS

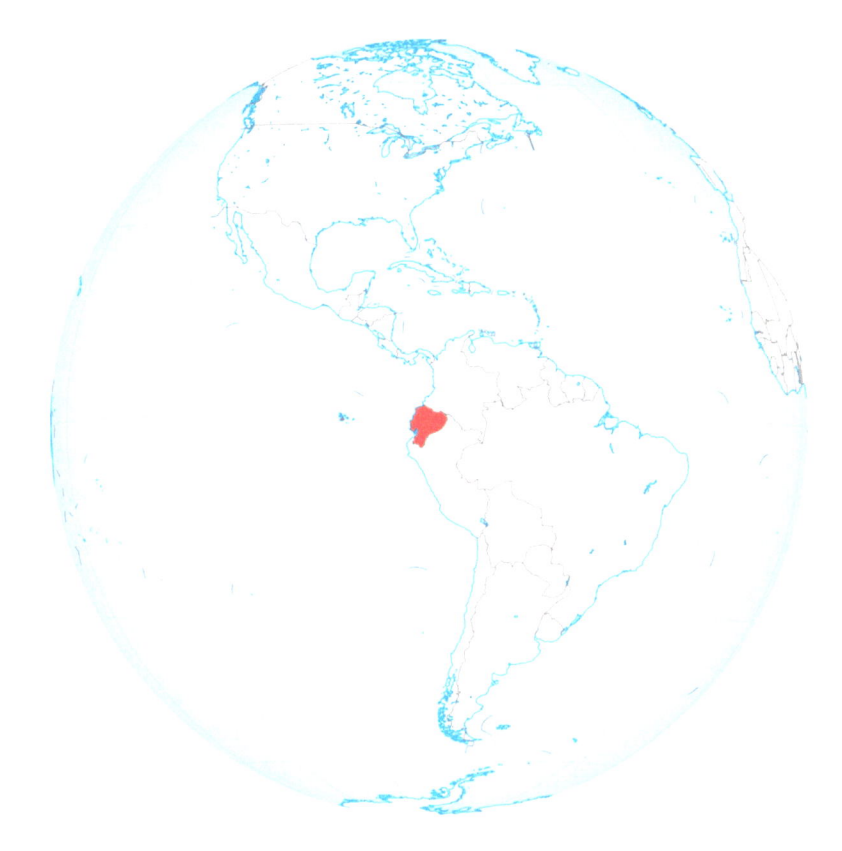

Day 397: Sunday, 10th April, 2005, Puerto Ayora

The wake-up call sounded shortly after ridiculous o'clock this morning. With a long day of logistics and, hopefully, travelling ahead of us, we forced ourselves out of bed and into action. It was still dark outside by the time we had packed and made our way down to the hotel lobby. The front desk receptionist was lying on the couch but woke up and got himself into gear when he heard us coming. I had to pay the US $40 (€30.77) we still owed for this past night's accommodation, but the checkout formalities were otherwise swiftly dealt with. I had ordered a taxi to take us to the airport, but a very comfortable private car showed up. The helpful driver did take care of our bags for us, though. I'd already been told the taxi arranged by the hotel would cost *nearly* US $5

(€3.85), so I just handed the man a US $5 note when we arrived at the airport. He was happy with that.

The domestic terminal at Quito's Mariscal Sucre International Airport was bustling that morning, with barely enough space to walk around. Luckily, very few people were at the ticket counter. I flashed my note with the name of the check-in supervisor with whom I spoke yesterday afternoon. They wanted me to go to the check-in desks, so I reluctantly shuffled my way through the throng to find it. When I arrived, the supervisor was there but working through a long row of people trying to check-in. I managed to grab the attention of the lady who was still there from yesterday. After spotting me, she picked up the phone and told me to return to the ticket desk. She called ahead to let them know I was coming. It seemed inefficient, but I would be happy to jump through their hoops if it meant getting us onto the flight.

At the ticket counter, again, I handed over our passports. The young lady went to work typing frantically on her terminal keyboard. I started to feel at ease for the first time that morning once I saw her feed a fresh flight coupon into the printer. She told me the total cost of those last-minute tickets would be US $390 (€300) per person for the return journey after including all the taxes.

I'd read on the Internet that the TAME airline discounted their tickets for students, so I took out my cards and asked if we would be eligible for such a discount. She studied the cards for a good couple of minutes. I was starting to worry that she might think they were fakes. She eventually returned them to me and shook her head as if to say that they weren't acceptable. I asked her what the problem was, and she called a supervisor. That worried me, but the supervisor, the first person we met today who spoke English, explained that there was a thirty-year-old age limit on the student discounts. Oh well; nothing ventured, nothing gained.

I wasn't particularly bothered about not getting the fifteen per cent student discount. As it was, I was relieved to get on the flight.

It wasn't long after checking in before we were all allowed to walk to our waiting Boeing 727 and find a seat for ourselves. With no assigned seating, I was glad we were among the first out of the door. That allowed us to locate a seat relatively close to the front row. There was no business class seating on the flight. I almost lost Sandy before we even reached the Galápagos Islands. She got up and nearly left the plane at the brief stopover at Guayaquil. I might have forgotten to tell her about that stopover before we left.

We were bound for a small runway on Baltra, a small island just north of Santa Cruz. I could barely contain my excitement about finally arriving in the Galápagos Islands. In touching down, yet another lifelong dream and ambition had come true. It was a surreal moment for me. We'd seen some truly astonishing things throughout this trip, but in the back of my mind had always been the anticipation of what to expect when we finally made it to the Galápagos Islands. I'd long believed it would be the highlight of our entire travels for me. All those things I found fascinating, such as photography, wildlife, natural history, geology, and species evolution, could all be experienced, studied, or collectively enjoyed in this single location. The tiny archipelago was another example of a single location whose size was vastly disproportionate to its significance in the grand scheme.

The small airport at which we landed that morning sits on the tiny island of Baltra, which butts up to the bigger island of Santa Cruz, one of the larger islands in the group and home to the main settlement of Puerto Ayora. Most travellers to the Galápagos Islands end up there first.

As expected, the first thing we each had to do after clearing immigration was to pay our US $100 (€76.92) national park entrance fee. We then had to wait a while for the luggage to be brought into the small open-air building. Baltra was one of the few airports without a baggage belt. Instead, the bags were laid out in rows in a cordoned-off baggage claim area for the passengers to search through.

I was immediately on the lookout for touts from departing cruises, looking for arriving passengers. We planned to show up and try to organise a last-minute cruise on a boat looking to fill any remaining empty berths. That was supposed to be a much cheaper way of doing things. However, that approach brought the significant risk of simply not finding anything available, so we weren't out of the woods yet by a long shot.

Just one boat representative was there calling for arriving passengers. He didn't seem interested, so we'd have to see what we could arrange when we got into Puerto Ayora. One of several small booths near the baggage claim area was the ticket counter for the coach trip into town. I bought our US $1.80 (€1.38) tickets, and we loaded ourselves onto the waiting claptrap of a coach.

The kid who sold me the bus tickets didn't mention that the trip to Puerto Ayora was a three-step journey. The bus took us to a ferry that took us to another bus. The ferry was to get us from Baltra to Santa Cruz Island. We unloaded our bags from the first bus and onto the roof of the ferry, after which the ten or fifteen of us boarded the lower deck of the small, open ferry for the five-minute crossing to the main island of Santa Cruz.

We were already starting to see some fascinating birds and fish in the crystal-clear waters around us. We were each relieved of another US 80¢ (61¢) for the brief ferry crossing, but our bus tickets were still valid for the second and longer bus journey on the other side. Taxi touts were busy trying to sell their US $25 (€19.23) rides into town, but everyone got onto the next waiting coach. There were more locals than tourists on that journey into town. I hoped that the lack of tourist numbers was a good indication there might be some berth availability on at least some boats.

On the one-hour bus ride up and over the island of Santa Cruz, we met and started chatting with an Australian girl. Like us, she was travelling to the Galápagos Islands for the first time. She, too, was winging it and hoping to find a last-minute deal. She had set herself a budget of US $500 (€384.61). Since we were all in the same boat together (literally), we decided to pool our resources when we arrived. I kept my eyes peeled as our bus struggled to make its way up and over the centre of the island's land mass towards Puerto Ayora on its Southern edge. The island juts out of the ocean to a peak of around 2,430 m (7,976 feet), so it was quite a climb to get over the top to the other side. Unlike Tahiti, another roughly round island, there was no coast road encircling the island — just the single road that roughly dissects it from Batra in the North to Puerto Ayora, the main settlement on the island, in the South. Other than the occasional birds, there wasn't a lot of wildlife to see throughout the arduous bus ride. The island was covered in shrub vegetation.

When the bus finally pulled in and dropped us off, the three of us decided that Sandy would guard the backpacks at a nearby café while the Australian girl and I went off to explore the tiny town and discuss organising a cruise.

We'd barely made it across the street when a short and tubby tout stood up and asked us if we were looking for a last-minute cruise deal. Since we were, we went with him to his nearby office. However, my traveller's instincts told me not to trust this character. I'd come to trust my gut instincts in such matters. The second flight of the day wasn't due to arrive for some time, so it didn't seem like a few minutes to hear what he had to say would cost us anything. Accordingly, we accompanied him to his office, where he tried to sell us a berth on a boat departing the next day.

There were four categories of cruise vessels sailing around the islands. Those were Economy, Tourist-Economy, Tourist-Superior and Luxury. According to Freddy (even the name sounded shady), we could purchase a seven-day cruise on a Tourist-Economy boat for US $600 (€461.52). That all sounded nearly too good to be true, so alarm bells constantly rang in my head. The boat was not there now, which also concerned me. He told me I could pay him US $50 (€38.46) to secure the berth, but he also suggested we could see the boat and talk to the departing passengers when it arrived tonight. He would refund the deposit if we weren't satisfied after seeing the vessel.

One of my concerns about the whole thing was that there would only be a level II guide on board as opposed to a level III. I was specifically looking for a cruise with a level III guide since those were both multi-lingual and formerly educated in the natural sciences. Freddy tried to tell me there were almost no level III guides on any of the boats. That didn't seem to tally with all the advice I'd previously received about ensuring we secured a cruise with a level III guide. Things didn't seem to add up very well with Freddy. Neither of us was particularly bowled over by this guy. What finally put the final nail into his coffin for me was that he kept insisting he was trustworthy. That was never a good sign. We told him we would need to think things over and left.

Our guidebook suggested several places in town where we could go to see about arranging last-minute deals. The first we tried was near the harbour, but the Spanish-speaking girl there didn't seem to have anything for us. We went farther into town to a second, where a couple of young women, who also spoke only Spanish, sat at a couple of desks inside an unlikely-looking shack. Even though neither the Australian girl nor I knew any more than the odd word of Spanish, those two girls clearly must have arranged those last-minute cruises for people all the time. We were strangely quite successful at communicating our needs to them. They had a couple of options that would suit our timelines, but the one that seemed the most interesting was the NEMO I catamaran. Quite surprisingly, for such a large vessel, it only accommodated twelve passengers with a half dozen private berths, each with an en-suite bathroom and air-conditioning. It was a Tourist-Superior class vessel. From what I could tell from the pictures and description, it seemed like a charming boat indeed. At US $1,300 (€1,000) per person for the eight-day itinerary, however, it was a big price difference compared to what our Freddy was offering for the same boat class.

We spent well over an hour trying to ask questions about the boat and the itinerary, but there were some finer details we couldn't clarify due to the communication barrier. Eventually, all four of us resorted to stopping passers-by on the street to ask them if they spoke both English and Spanish and were able to help with a bit of translation. It took several passers-by before we stopped an extremely accommodating older man who spoke both languages. He turned out to be a former member of the board of tourism for the Galápagos Islands. I asked him to ask the girls to explain why there might be such a big difference in price between the NEMO I and the other boat that Freddy was offering.

When he learnt which Freddy I was referring to, he immediately reacted. Our Freddy was apparently indeed a very shoddy operator, according to this man. While this guy was on the tourism board, he'd personally received more complaints about Freddy and his activities than anyone else. I was glad my instincts were vindicated.

This friendly man spent a few minutes helping us with our translation needs. He confirmed that the NEMO I was an exceptionally well-recommended boat and assured us that we would enjoy our cruise aboard. His parting advice was not to do business with Freddy but to enjoy our trip aboard the NEMO I. That clinched it for me. If the NEMO I was good enough for a respected member of the tourism board for the Galápagos Islands, it would certainly be good enough for us.

Since the list price for the eight-day cruise aboard the NEMO I was no less than US $1,700 (€1307.70), it seemed like we were also getting that last-minute bargain we came. At that point, one of the local dive masters came in. He, too, confirmed we were fortunate to get a berth aboard that catamaran. For the ten minutes he was in the shack, he also helped with translation.

I didn't fully understand how or why, but while he was there, the price had dropped from US $1,300 (€1,000) to just US $1,200 (€923). Bonus!

I also spent some time negotiating something for the Australian woman. She was more than happy to allow me to drive the negotiating process on her behalf and confessed she was much less well-informed than she thought I was. Although above her initially set budget, all the positive press we had just gotten about the NEMO I and the now US $1,200 (€923) cost of the private air-conditioned berth seemed to do the trick for her. She, too, booked one of the last places on the vessel.

She had to go across the street to the town's only bank to withdraw some money, so I went back to collect the cash Sandy had buried in her backpack and explain to her where we'd been for the past hour.

On the way, I stopped at one of the hotels in town to find a room. Puerto Ayora had several hostels and backpacker joints, but I decided to fork out the extra for a more comfortable room with air conditioning. It was hot and humid, and it was, after all, the end of our trip. There was less pressing need to be so tight-fisted with the budget now that the end was in sight.

I settled on two nights in one of the better places in town, the Hotel Lobo Del Mar, for a total of US $141 (€108.46). That would cover us until our cruise commenced. Sandy must have wondered just where I was all that time. When I returned to where we'd left her, she had already met another couple of Canadian travellers and was happily chatting with them. I collected all the ready cash we had accumulated and went back to make payment for our cruise. I took some of our bags to drop off at the hotel on the way to save time and energy. With the heat and stifling humidity, I didn't want Sandy to carry anything heavy.

With the cruise and our accommodation settled, I was a very happy camper and returned to join Sandy at the café for lunch. As we sat there waiting for our food to come out, the Australian girl came to collect her bags, which Sandy had been babysitting. Whilst at the bank, she had chatted with someone there. They confirmed to her that the NEMO I was a great boat and that the one Freddy was trying to sell us berths on was an over-packed cockroach-ridden safety hazard waiting to sink. It was one of three boats owned by the same people who had allowed maintenance and standards to go downhill. We all felt contented about the morning's progress we'd made.

After finishing our lunch, we said a temporary goodbye to our new Australian friend and took the rest of our bags to the hotel. I was excited about our upcoming cruise and popped into the booking office several times throughout the afternoon to ask the girls more questions. I also wanted to ask them what we could get up to today and tomorrow to kill time.

We could do several things, but they involved lots of walking around in the heat and humidity. Given Sandy's pregnancy, they suggested we check out the nearby Charles Darwin Research Institute, where several Galápagos tortoise and iguana enclosures were easy to visit and didn't require strenuous activity.

We hailed one of the dozens of white pickup trucks that perused the streets. For the fixed rate of US $1 (77¢) per ride within town, we were whisked the kilometre or so over there.

The institute was an extremely worthy research centre. Endangered Galápagos turtles and other threatened species were bred there in captivity to be released back into the wild. That was an ongoing effort to undo the damage done to this precious ecosystem by man over the past couple of hundred years.

We weren't allowed into any of the several larger buildings where the research was carried out, but there were several walkthrough enclosures where giant tortoises were kept in small groups. That was our first real up-close encounter with a Galápagos species, and it was a pretty memorable experience for both of us.

They also had a range of Galápagos iguanas in separate enclosures. Different sub-species had different colourations. The Yellow Land Iguana was especially impressive.

Even more impressive were the several bird species we noticed perched on trees and handrails throughout the park. The animals on the Galápagos Islands evolved without man or any other predators. The islands were too far from the mainland for predatory animals to have made the journey. As such, the local wildlife evolved without the instinctive fear usually present in animals from elsewhere in the world. The absence of that fear and flight instinct meant we could get extraordinarily close to the birds without them flying away.

As we walked around, we bumped into another couple of travellers led by a private guide. We asked the older guide a few questions. He was charming and informative. In retrospect, I wished we had such a guide to help explain everything we saw as we walked around. He also confirmed that the NEMO I was a great boat. Coincidentally, the level III guide accompanying us on our cruise was his cousin.

After a fascinating few hours at the research station admiring the tortoises, iguanas, and birds, we slowly strolled back into town, stopping in at a couple of shops along the way. I picked up a nice map of the islands with some helpful bird and animal photos we could use for identification.

Although we'd now paid in full for our cruise, I also hoped to do some diving. I still needed to pay for those dives, so we collected our traveller's checks from the hotel and went to cash them all in at the one bank on the island.

We first tried to use our bank cards at the island's only ATM, but none of them worked. That was the reason we had the traveller's checks as a fallback. The bank was heaving with a long, bendy line of customers, probably because today was payday. There was a smaller queue in the pregnant women's line, so we joined that one. I knew Sandy's condition would come in handy eventually.

The bank charged me US $5 (€3.85) as a flat rate for cashing the traveller's checks, but I could cash all the remaining US $400 (€307.69) we had in checks.

Whilst out and about, we bumped into the Canadian couple Sandy had met in the café when I was working my magic sorting out a cruise. We agreed to go out for dinner together that evening. I had already asked the pleasant young girl at our hotel's reception desk where to go for a delicious meal. She advised a small place a short way up the coast that was only reachable via a water taxi.

It was dusk by now, and we had all boarded the small taxi before I realised I didn't know the name of the restaurant where we had made our booking. None of us spoke Spanish, and the water taxi driver certainly didn't speak English, so I just motioned my hand towards my mouth to suggest eating. There must only have been one restaurant reachable via the water tax. Our driver immediately pulled away from the dock and took us several hundred metres to where a restaurant protruded over the water's edge.

They had been expecting us, so we were at least at the right place. Judging by the price and neatly presented small portions we were served, it was a very upscale restaurant. The food was delicious. We ended up paying US $48 (€36.92) for what surely would have cost over four times that much anywhere else. Even though the meal was a fantastic bargain, it was still much more than we were accustomed to paying for a single meal on the road. I was still very much in the mood to disregard the budget completely.

We enjoyed the meal and the company immensely. However, it made for a later evening than we were accustomed to. I was so tired when we returned to the hotel that I could only write brief notes to capture the day's activities before nodding off. I often did that during our travels. I always wrote a whole journal entry for each day just before sleeping. Sometimes, I had to manage with just a brief series of reminders so that I could complete the journal entry the following day. Before doing so, we had a quick tally of the cash we still had. We thought we were missing a big chunk of money for a while. It turned out I had lost track of when and where we had been spending cash. Whichever way we cut it, we were still going to come in well under budget for Ecuador and the Galápagos islands.

Day 398: Monday, 11th April, 2005, Puerto Ayora

Yesterday was such a late night, so we chose to sleep in this morning rather than get up early enough for breakfast. By the time we mobilised, we were starting to wonder what to do with ourselves for the day. Not knowing our options, we thought we'd check around town for a private guide for a half-day. That didn't seem like it would be difficult, so we decided to sort that out before getting breakfast.

As it turned out, many of the booking offices around town were closed today. We walked up and down the town's main commercial street, thoroughly exhausting ourselves — precisely what I had wanted to avoid. Most of the morning, then, was spent unproductively.

Even after following the advice of our hotel's receptionist, we only found one place that was open and willing to entertain the idea of locating a private guide for the day. He first suggested we spend the afternoon exploring the highlands in the island's centre. There were lava tubes and wild Galápagos tortoises to be enjoyed in that part of the island.

The girls at the booking office where I had booked our cruise had told me a tour of the highlands would likely be included in the cruise itinerary, so he then suggested a place just around the coast called Tortuga Bay. The only problem with that idea was that it required a one-hour trek to get there and another one-hour trek to get back. As it turned out, Tortuga Bay was where a twelve-year-old girl drowned just a few days ago. There was a huge and pristine white sand beach there, which was very good for snorkelling. Just past the sandbanks, however, there were rip tides and heavy surf that could quickly cause problems. As was the case with Freddy from yesterday, I was starting to get the impression we weren't going to be doing ourselves a favour by booking a guide with this guy, so we told him we would think about his offer of a guide for US $40 (€30.77) for a couple of hours in the afternoon and get back to him.

By now, it was lunchtime, so we wandered around looking for a place to eat where we could speak with an English-speaking server or read from an English-written menu. We weren't successful in that endeavour, and fatigue finally got the best of us. We settled for the same café where we ate yesterday morning. Their hash brown, eggs and bacon breakfast sounded like it would go down well. It did look very appetising when it finally came out. However, the chef decided to throw in a slice of cheese, so I had to return it for another plate.

As we sat and ate, another couple entered the open-air dining area. We quickly struck up a conversation with them. It was another Canadian couple visiting for just a few days, trying to tackle the islands through day trips and excursions rather than a cruise.

We had struck out finding a guide for the afternoon, so we said goodbye to the Canadians and went back to our hotel to rest during the hottest part of the day.

The Internet terminal was available, so we looked at the website the two girls at the booking office had told us about yesterday. Although we'd seen a small photo of the NEMO I, this was our first real look at the huge catamaran and its innards. We were delighted by what we saw.

More than ever, we were looking forward to our cruise tomorrow morning.

The exact itinerary was also posted on the website. I was interested to note that the only activity listed while the vessel was docked in Puerto Ayora was the Charles Darwin Research Institute, not the highlands tour. We could salvage the afternoon after all by taking that tour today.

Since we had no luck locating a guide via the booking offices in town, we might not get that chance. Then I remembered the charming guide we met yesterday. I pondered the idea of being able to hire him for the afternoon. The problem was that we didn't know who he was or how we could reach him. I remembered the couple we had seen him with yesterday would be diving this morning with a dive outfit close to the research institute. I knew that because the guide had half suggested we join them this morning. I declined the offer, knowing I would be too tired to get out of bed at six o'clock this morning.

Armed with that information, I strolled over to the dive office in the hope that the staff there might know how to contact that couple so that I could ask them how they managed to secure the services of their guide. The woman at the dive office and I tried to identify which couple it could have been. Without any names to go on, she was trying to remember who went on the morning dive based on my description.

As we did that, they returned from their dive, so I asked them directly. It turned out that the guide was from their hotel in the middle of the island. He was already giving a tour that morning. With their help, I located the guide's mobile phone number, so I took that with me to search for a phone to call him from.

I first tried our hotel's reception desk, but they apparently could not call mobile phones. I was more successful from an Internet café just around the corner, and I managed to reach him.

The connection was abysmal, but he did promise to call me back at the hotel to discuss our needs further. That he did. However, after all the effort, he was unavailable as he was already giving another tour. I explained to him that I had learnt that our cruise itinerary did not include the Santa Cruz Highland tour. He said he'd call his cousin, our cruise guide, to verify on which day the NEMO I would be docked at Santa Cruz. He suggested that we could hire him on that day to visit the highlands while the rest of the passengers were visiting the research institute, which we had already done.

That sounded like an excellent idea, and I was thankful he was so obliging. It wasn't often we met someone willing to go so far out of their way to be so accommodating. I hoped we would get the chance to spend some time with him and learn about the wildlife of Santa Cruz at some point during our cruise.

That evening would likely be the last chance to pick up a few souvenirs from the Galápagos Islands, so we ventured out into town to explore the shops and see what was on offer. Every shop there sold a similar array of t-shirts and trinkets based on the shapes of the typical animals found on and around the archipelago.

Mangroves grew rampant around the various island's coastlines. A fungus grew on the mangroves, which was harvested, dried, and carved into Galápagos animal forms. Harvesting the fungus didn't damage or harm the ecosystem in any way, and the resulting sculptures were unique keepsakes, so we found a couple that we liked from the one shop in town selling them. We picked up a t-shirt and, of course, a carved wooden Galápagos tortoise. Sandy also picked up some Galápagos animal bracelet pendants.

While shopping for souvenirs, we bumped into the second Canadian couple we had met earlier. We discovered we were all planning to eat at the same restaurant that evening, so we agreed to meet there at seven o'clock.

After finishing off our shopping, we made our way to the Red Mango restaurant, located, quite literally, in the middle of a mangrove forest right next to the waterfront. The annoying mosquitoes confirmed the location, but when we turned up, we found the second Canadian couple we had expected and the first Canadian couple with whom we had eaten last night. The four of them sat at a table for six with our two places waiting for us.

It was a Japanese menu. I picked out the grilled eel to be a bit adventurous. It was delicious, and we enjoyed a long evening of mutually good company. The bill for the two of us was US $33 (€25.38). We had a lot of fun, and the evening continued for some time. Yet again, we would return to our hotel much later than we might have.

Day 399: Tuesday, 12th April, 2005, NEMO I

We skipped what we anticipated would be a very meagre breakfast that morning and instead took time to pack and get our act together. I'd already paid in full for our two nights of accommodation when we first checked in, so we hailed a taxi outside to take us to the bus station for our trip back to Baltra and the start of our long-awaited Galápagos cruise.

I made sure to clearly articulate the required destination of the bus station to the driver. We thought he instantly knew what we meant, but for some reason, he took us to a nearby hotel instead. We had to draw upon our recently acquired phrasebook to get him to understand precisely where we needed to go. How we got Bus Station and Hotel Galápagos mixed up wasn't clear, but that was the ever-present communication barrier at work again.

We got there in the end and handed over the standard fare of US $1 (77¢). Karen, the Australian girl who had booked onto the same boat as us, was already at the bus station. We chatted to kill time before buying our US $1.80 (€1.38) bus tickets and climbing aboard. I, for one, was glad to be on the bus and no longer out in the open. The thousands of small and incessant flies were buzzing around. They weren't the sort that bit or stung, but they did swarm around the face and eyes and were infuriating if we stopped moving.

The bus took us the now familiar hour route over the island to the dock, where we were to board the small ferry back to Baltra. As we boarded the ferry, we were treated to a remarkable phenomenon. A massive flock of hundreds, if not thousands, of blue-footed boobies, were circling the waters in a low pattern. Now and then, they darted swiftly into the water like missiles. As one dived, the rest all followed suit. The impact of hundreds of them entering the water quickly sounded like a machine gun was firing.

Blue-footed boobies have long and pointed bills. They hit the water after bending back their wings, converting themselves into a pointed spear. Their speed as they hit the water carries them on for several metres as they slice through the water, hunting for fish.

One by one, they all swiftly popped their heads out of the water, shook themselves dry and took off again for another pass over the water. It was impressive enough to see that behaviour from an individual bird, but this collective effort of targeting schools of small fish by hundreds of them at a time in a diving frenzy was astonishing. Our cruise hadn't even started, but I already thought today was a big success for us, having witnessed such an incredible spectacle.

After the mass booby-feeding frenzy, I was on a high for quite a while. Before I knew it, we had pulled up to the airport without me realising we had already completed the second shorter bus journey.

The three of us were expecting to find our guide or some other representative from our cruise company waiting for us, but we didn't see anything that looked obvious when we got off the bus. Quite a few people were arriving and departing the small airport, so we may have missed him in the chaos.

Sandy and Karen sat with the bags while I went to find him. He was searching for some passengers from one of the recently arrived flights. It turned out not to be the guide we expected. Another had been arranged at the last minute because our intended guide had to pull out. Our replacement guide, Juan Carlos, was a level III naturalist guide with over twenty years of experience. I knew we'd be in good hands with him.

We had to wait around for about an hour while the remainder of the passengers on our cruise arrived on the next couple of incoming flights. In the meantime, we did some more last-minute souvenir shopping. Sandy bought herself a better hat. Once we had all assembled our bags, we made our way to the nearby cruise boat dock in a truck and then a bus.

The cruise boat dock was just a few minutes drive from the airport. As soon as we arrived, we started to see a wealth of Galápagos wildlife. In addition to the sea lions lazing under the jetty, we saw several birds, including frigates soaring overhead.

Our vessel stood out amongst the crowd, being the only catamaran in the water. Our boat's small launch, known locally as a panga, arrived to collect us all. It swiftly took us over to greet the NEMO I for the first time.

Our guide, Juan, wasted no time initiating his boat safety and Galápagos conservation briefing.

The NEMO I was quite a fantastic vessel. We would enjoy ourselves immensely over the coming week getting to know it well. All was not a bed of roses, however. A couple of significant differences emerged between what we were told was part of the deal and what had turned out to be the case. Less significantly, although still quite annoying, we were informed that water and soft drinks were included in the package and that alcohol was extra. However, we were now told that soft drinks were extra, too. Since we tend to drink a lot of soft drinks, that wasn't particularly welcome news. Even though every other passenger was also under the same impression of complimentary soft drinks on board, it remained the apparent policy of the cruise company to not include them for free.

I could live with the extra dollar here and there for a soft drink, but more of an issue was that we were led to believe the cabins were spacious and air-conditioned. The cabin quarters were quite tight and cramped, and the boat had no air conditioning. That last issue didn't sit well with me at all. I made my dissatisfaction very plain to our guide and the boat owner, who just happened to spend the afternoon with us on this first day. I felt cheated in not receiving what I was told we were paying for. To be fair, the misrepresentation of expectations probably wasn't the owner's fault. They were likely just as annoyed as we were.

Shortly after the initial boat briefing, a lunch of braised meat, salad, and fruit was served. As part of the initial briefing, we had to confirm our dietary wishes and requirements. It would be interesting to see how well we fared with the food onboard for the coming week.

During lunch, the catamaran idled from the channel where the dock resided, out around the island to our first destination. A pristine, white-sand beach was to be our first disembarkation point. There were to be two types of landing. This first one was a wet landing. The panga took us all a few hundred metres to shore, where we had to jump over the side into knee-deep water to reach the beach.

There was a wealth of wildlife on this sandy shore, much of it unique to this location. For starters, numerous bright red and yellow crabs scurried around the beach, making for fantastic photography. Their bright colours contrasted beautifully against the white sand's background.

We also saw a marine iguana and several interesting birds, such as the American Oystercatcher.

The waves crashed gently against a rising bank of powdery sand beach that rose inland to form a ridgeline around the shore. At the top of this ridge were dozens of steaks marking the sites of turtle nests. This was the time of year when turtles returned to their birthplaces to lay hundreds of eggs in nests on the sand beaches where they were born.

We'd have little chance of seeing the turtles themselves, however, since there was a land curfew throughout the Galápagos Islands between the hours of sunset and sunrise. That was one of many rules and regulations to protect and preserve the fragile environment.

We enjoyed a good hour on the beach, photographing the wildlife before our panga came to collect us and ferry us back to the catamaran. A couple of us got the unique chance to be hoisted up to the top of the main sail mast to take photos of the boat below. That made for some stunning images.

The briefing for tomorrow's itinerary followed our dinner that evening. I was only now starting to relax a bit from my earlier bout of sulking due to the air-conditioning issue.

Day 400: Wednesday, 13th April, 2005, NEMO I

We've had restless nights throughout this round-the-world trip and for various reasons. However, I could honestly say we'd never had problems sleeping due to sea lions climbing over our roof and grunting at each other for half the night. That was precisely what happened last night. It wasn't every day that we could claim to be kept awake by the local sea lion population.

We were moored relatively close to a couple of landmasses throughout the night. To keep the mosquitoes away, we had to close the hatches to our cabins. Consequently, it was uncomfortably warm without air conditioning, which didn't help us get a good night's sleep either.

After breakfast, we were taken to the nearby island of North Seymour for the first of two guided excursions. That would be the format of the overall cruise: a couple of landings each day between meals on the NEMO I.

Some fifty-odd visitor sites were dotted around the Galápagos Islands, where cruise operators were allowed to land their passengers. Even though those stretched to nearly every island in the archipelago, only one per cent of the total landmass of the islands was directly affected. That included visiting tourists, permanent settlements, research stations and military installations. Even though that was a comforting thought, all the naturalist guides took great care to instil into every visitor the necessity and importance of minimising the impact of tourism. As nature lovers and wildlife enthusiasts, we were comforted by that.

From where we landed on Seymour Island, painted steaks were impaled into the ground, marking out trails where we were allowed to tread. Seymour had essentially one trail we could follow. We spent the better part of a couple of hours slowly following that trail while Juan Carlos took his time to tell us all about the island's wildlife and ecology.

We were fortunate to be visiting Seymour at this time of year. The blue-footed boobies and the frigate birds were courting and nesting there in colonies.

We saw hundreds of blue-footed boobies all over the island. Even though we remained within the metre and a half-width of the trails, we still had to move aside from time to time to avoid treading on them — that's how numerous they were.

The Blue-footed Boobies stood about 50 cm (20″) tall and were dotted around mostly in mating pairs. Both males and females performed their ritual mating dances by raising their blue webbed feet alternately into the air as they strutted around each other.

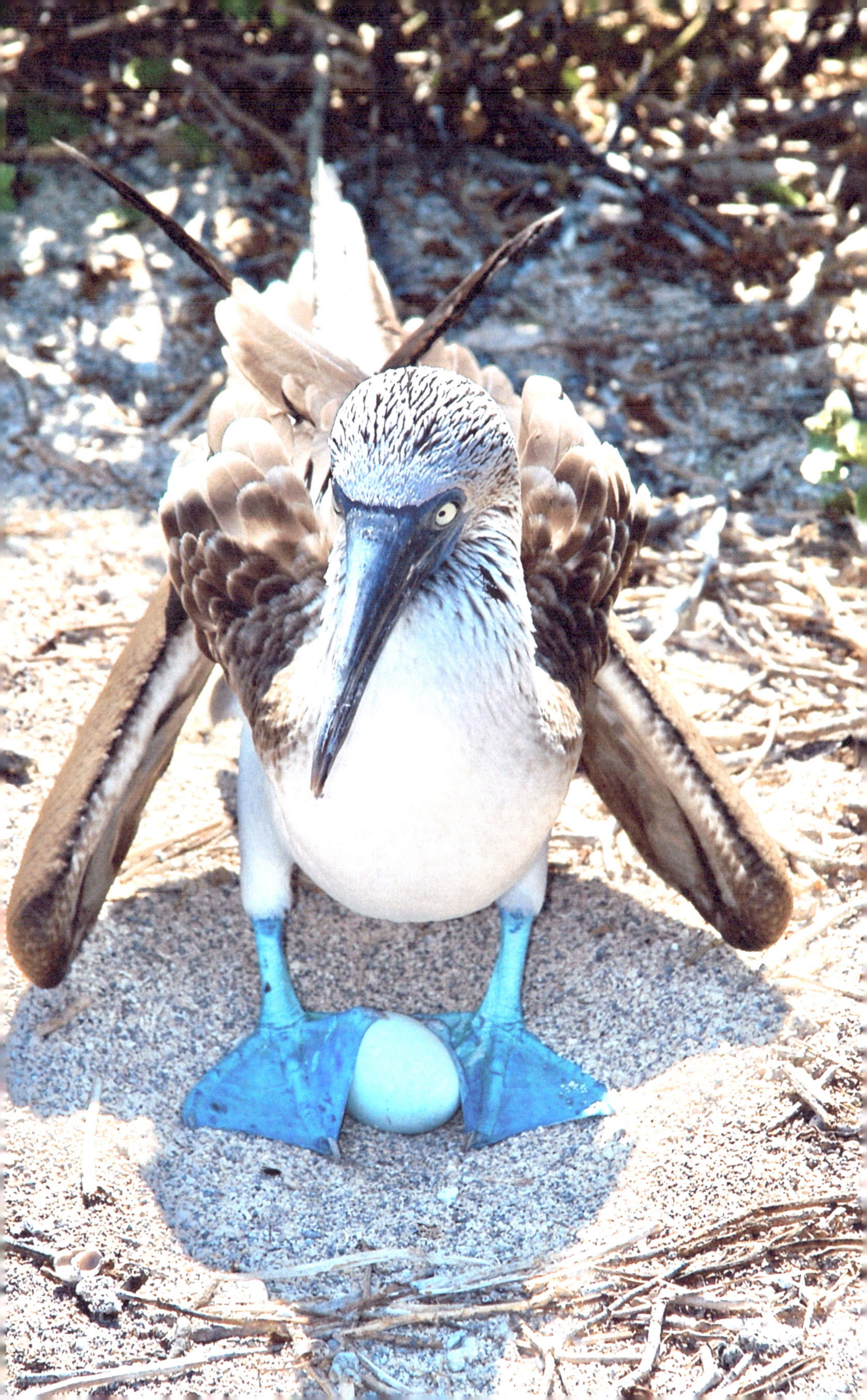

There are very few instances in the natural world where the colour blue is so vividly present. Those birds are the exception that proves the rule. They were very unlikely-looking animals indeed. Many of the boobies there were courting, but many also were brooding an individual egg, on which they held their webbed feet to keep the egg's temperature regulated.

Now and then, we'd see one of the parent birds stand up to gently roll the egg and then sit down on it again. It felt unusual to be able to get so close to the birds and other animals without them experiencing fear and fleeing. It was fascinating to witness the mating rituals and to see how one male encroaches upon another's territory, thus creating friction and scraps between them.

The blue-footed boobies were a real treat, but there were yet more fascinating spectacles awaiting us. North Seymour also happened to house a colony of frigate birds. Those were majestic and graceful birds flying above us almost everywhere since arriving on the archipelago.

They looked large while soaring through the air but were almost all skin, bones and feathers. They were incredibly light and could hover effortlessly in the air. What was most striking about the frigate was how the males attracted females whilst courting. Much like the pelican, the underside of the male jaw is very elastic. The bird could inflate its throat pouch like a giant balloon. When fully inflated, it was the most brilliant colour, red and nearly dwarfed the bird. Those frigates, too, were in various stages of their breeding cycle.

We were also fortunate to see several fluffy chicks perching on the low shrubs. I continued to be stunned at how close we could get to the birds without them flying away. In the case of the blue-footed boobies, they were sometimes standing or sitting right in the middle of the trails, forcing us to walk right past them to get through.

Juan Carlos was passionate about the Galápagos Islands and, more importantly, their protection. He was very strict about ensuring we all stayed within the posted areas. He even chastised members of other groups moving around the island whenever he saw someone straying from the paths. The guides could and did report other guides who did not keep a tight rein on their groups.

The island we visited that morning was also littered with countless land iguanas and the much smaller lava lizards. Those, too, had no fear for humans and made little attempt to move out of our way when we passed through.

The now familiar sea lions also sat in great numbers up and down the island's coast. Even those were remarkably unperturbed by our presence. Many of them were nursing young pups. Those playful little creatures were a lot of fun to watch frolicking around. The Galápagos land iguanas and lava lizards were in great numbers on the island but were different sub-species from those we'd seen before. The iguanas were reddish due to the other diets on North Seymour Island, and the lava lizards were slightly larger than their brethren. The females sported an orangey-red head and neck colouring.

Around the world OCEANIA & SOUTH AMERICA

We enjoyed walking around the island and spotting all the weird and wonderful prehistoric-like creatures we wouldn't see anywhere else. It was a good two and a half hours of slow walking in the middle of the day. By the time we had completed our circuit back to the panga, the sun was starting to get to us all.

We might have been able to go diving after lunch, but the water was very green and murky. Juan Carlos decided that the visibility would be insufficient and that getting into the water wouldn't have been worthwhile. Diving was on the agenda for tomorrow, so I could look forward to that.

Much of the afternoon was spent simply relaxing on the NEMO I. Everybody had their method of relaxing; some took to the sun deck whilst others went for a nap.

A few of us cracked open the backgammon board and a packet of cards. I introduced several people to the joys of Whist. Juan Carlos posted the day's agenda on a whiteboard for each day. To infuse a bit of extra activity into the schedule, he offered everyone a ride around the island in the panga. Most accepted the offer, but Sandy was still napping, and I wanted to pace myself for the long afternoon hike ahead of us.

Our second excursion was to the relatively small island of South Plaza. It started at sea level and slowly rose from the ground towards the far side, then dropped immediately back to the sea at a series of sheer cliffs. There were lots of large cactus trees, but the island was, for the most part, an open expanse of very low-lying grasses and shrubs.

Some recent rain had caused much of the low-lying vegetation to blossom into a sea of yellow flowers. We could see hundreds of the yellowish land iguanas out sunning themselves as far as the eye could see, occasionally feeding from the yellow flowers that had burst into life. We could see them stationary or crawling slowly towards the beach everywhere we looked.

We were excited to see the odd iguana close to us when we first got off the panga. By the time we were through with our guided hike, we were no longer trying to photograph them all the time. We also tried our best to avoid stepping on them as we walked.

When we reached the cliff face, we saw many more marine iguanas clinging to the rocks and sunning themselves. The updraft across the face of the cliff allowed birds to soar over the edge effortlessly. We enjoyed listening to Juan Carlos point out the various species.

Many of the birds were agile and extremely fast in the air. I had difficulty getting a good shot at them as they flew past. It wasn't just in the air that I had to point the camera either; we saw several schools of large fish in the waters below us. A beautiful spotted eagle ray also swam close to the water's surface.

The marine iguanas sitting on the rocks all around us differed from the land iguanas in various ways. They looked like they were the same animal except for their skin pigmentation. Marine iguanas hunted for their food beneath the waves. That was unique to the Galápagos Marine Iguana. They could hold their breath for about an hour while swimming out to forage for their favourite type of algae growing on the rocks up to 30 m (98 feet) deep in offshore waters. After eating and returning to dry land, they expelled salt water by sneezing from time to time. Also, the marine iguanas huddled together at night in groups to keep warm, whereas the land iguanas returned to their burrows in the ground where they nested.

On our way back to where our panga had dropped us off, we had to pass through the area where the sea lions were sunbathing. We had to walk around them as we passed. Juan Carlos got several of the pups going by imitating the call of an adult female. He got on his knees and had one of the pups come up to him to kiss him.

Once again, it was a spectacular hike and highly informative. However, we eventually had to return to the NEMO I.

The golden red sunset was magnificent as we all sat before the laptop to enjoy an impromptu slideshow of our day's photography. That evening, we set course for the southern tip of the archipelago. Depending on the currents, that would take anywhere from six to twelve hours of cruising against the wind. We would likely be cruising all through the night. I wasn't complaining. It meant we'd be well out of reach of mosquitoes and other bugs. We could leave our hatch open to allow fresher and cooler air to circulate around the cabin.

I had been enjoying the cruise immensely so far. However, the cramped and hot conditions of the boat didn't make me eager to recommend it to subsequent travellers.

The crew had arranged shrimp for dinner that evening. Sandy didn't eat fish, so the chef prepared a filet mignon for her. I managed to get wind of that early enough to request the same for myself. We both got a few jealous looks and comments from one or two of the other passengers. The meat was quite tough, and although it looked like filet mignon, the similarities with the succulent dish ended there. We'd come to have lower expectations of the food on the boat so far. That wasn't to say that the cook didn't do his level best to prepare a wide variety of good food; it was just that we were both very particular about what we would and wouldn't eat. Most of the other passengers had been perfectly happy with the very well-presented meals that had been prepared.

The evening was rounded off with Juan Carlos putting tomorrow's schedule on the whiteboard while briefing everyone on what to expect. From what I could gather, the format of one morning and one afternoon hike around one or more of the islands would be the format for the rest of the trip. Apart from just a couple of other passengers, everyone on board was a nature enthusiast. We eagerly anticipated visiting all the islands and seeing the differences between the wildlife and ecology between them. Since there would be diving opportunities tomorrow morning, our first hike would be at six o'clock. Accordingly, a five-thirty wake-up bell was scheduled. Almost everyone was in bed and off to sleep early that evening, preparing for the early start.

Day 401: Thursday, 14th April, 2005, NEMO I

It was still dark when the hideously early five-thirty wake-up bell was rung this morning. Most people had a much easier night this time since we were on the move to the island of Española in the far Southeast of the archipelago throughout the night. That made for a nice cool breeze and, perhaps more importantly, no mosquitoes, flies, or other bugs to keep us all awake.

Since it was such an early start to the day, breakfast was not yet being served, but the crew did lay out some biscuits, tea, and coffee for everyone. I hadn't especially enjoyed the food on the cruise so far, but it had been well prepared and very nicely presented. Nobody else had complained about the food, so I'd put it down to me being finicky.

Everyone assembled in the panga, and we set off for our guided hike around Punta Suez, a scenic hotspot for birdwatching on the island. The one thing that we immediately took note of after landing on the island was the multitudes of iguanas. They were of a slightly different variety. Although very similar in shape and size, they were a different colour. Depending on their gender, they were either a reddish colour or a near green or turquoise. Juan Carlos explained that the variation in the colour of the iguanas between islands was due to the different diets available to them locally.

We saw plenty of the now-familiar lava lizards throughout the hike, which also differed slightly from those we'd seen on previous islands. The females sported a brilliant orange colour around the head and neck. Unlike other animal species in the Galápagos Islands and elsewhere, those female lava lizards initiated the mating rituals and thus had that brightly coloured display. Ordinarily, the male of a given species tried to attract the females, but with lava lizards, things worked the other way around.

Although we had a very early start, we were still not the first to land on the island. We were just beaten to it by a party from one of the other boats in the bay. After we landed, we had to hang around for a few minutes to allow the group in front of us to move ahead.

A few mockingbirds were scurrying around our feet as we stood there waiting. They were looking for fresh water and somehow seemed to know we each had a bottle with us. Juan Carlos would not allow us to give them water, but it seemed clear from the bird's behaviour that people had done that in the past. The birds instinctively pecked at the bottle tops when offered to them. Allowing the birds to sip our water quickly taught them that was the easy way to find it. That could be a severe problem for the birds, who then fail to locate their water using natural means. Even that kind of innocent interference could have disastrous consequences for wildlife.

We've been fortunate in many respects with the timing of this cruise. Both the blue-footed boobies and the frigate birds had been in mating season, and we'd seen them in the various stages of courting, mating, brooding eggs, and rearing their chicks.

It also just so happened that the Galápagos albatrosses had just recently arrived and had started their courting and breeding season. We saw dozens of individual and mating pairs of albatrosses on the island, including a whole colony, at what Juan Carlos described as their landing site.

Albatrosses spent most of their lives at sea, only coming to land to mate and rear their young. They could spend incredibly long periods — weeks and even months — on the wing and are graceful birds in the air. As a result, their feet and legs are not particularly well suited to landing and walking, and they are disadvantaged in this area. For all their grace and beauty in the air, they are clumsy and cumbersome on the ground. We were very fortunate to see a couple of albatrosses copulating.

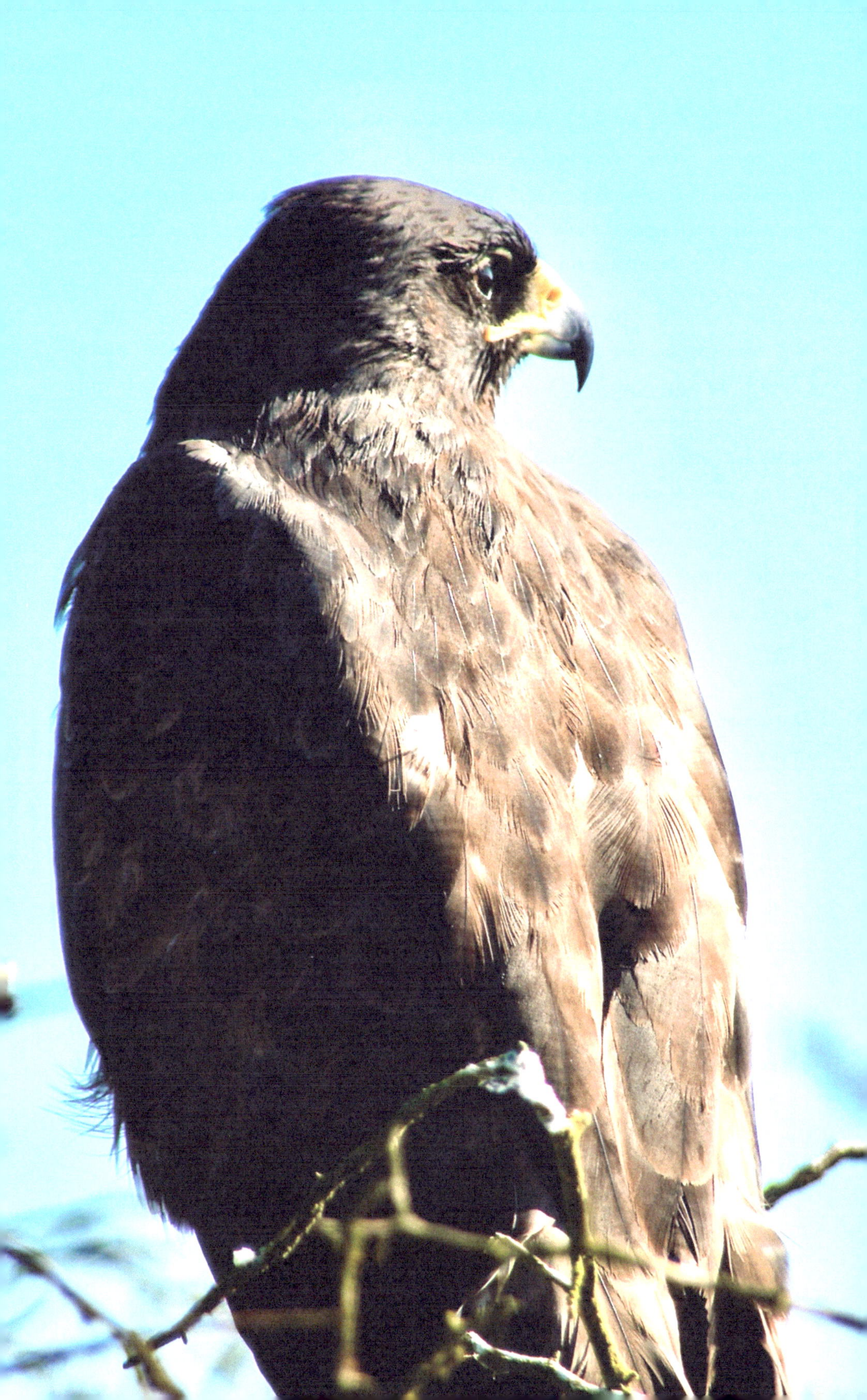

The albatrosses were a real treat, but the island was also home to one the largest colony of blue-footed boobies. We walked through an area that housed thousands, most of whom were courting and dancing for each other. Many of them were also sitting on eggs. We found at least a couple of birds sitting on multiple eggs.

As if the albatrosses and blue-footed boobies weren't enough, there was also a vast colony of Nazca boobies. There are three types of booby commonly found around the Galápagos Islands. We wouldn't be visiting any of the islands where the other common sort, the red-footed booby, could be found. The Nazca boobies must have recently had their mating season since we saw lots of their chicks and juveniles.

The trail around the island was extremely rocky and uneven. The whole island was strewn with boulders overgrown with bush and vegetation. The hiking path we followed had been cleared of vegetation. There was no other interference by man save for a few posts here and there to mark the boundaries of the path. Once again, Juan Carlos was emphatic about everybody, in our group or not, remaining within the limits of those staked posts.

The Olympus camera we had with us for SCUBA diving was still in the underwater housing from the previous dive, so we only had the Nikon with us today. We still managed to rack up 340 shots, though. With just one camera between us, we had to devise a means of sharing to avoid arguments, so we each used it every alternate half hour.

One side of the island sported a cliff-face edge with rocky outcroppings. The entire cliff area was littered with boobies, frigates, soaring albatrosses and other birds. We sat there for a while, happily watching them fly right over our heads. I was in photographic heaven as the albatrosses occasionally flew close to us.

A fissure in the rock kept erupting below us and just above sea level. Each time the huge sea swells crashed against the rocks, water was forced through a blowhole up to 30 m (100 feet) in height. From what we could see from the crystal-clear waters, the diving should be great later that morning.

Breakfast that morning was at eight forty-five. It was hard to believe we'd already had such a packed day of exploration by the time we ate. The captain set sail for our next destination around the island's far side as soon as the breakfast table was cleared.

As we sailed, those of us who would participate in the SCUBA diving started to sort out all the gear, trying various things on for size. Excluding Juan Carlos as our dive master, four divers would participate in the morning dive. As far as I could see, there was only enough equipment for five divers with no spares. That became an issue when we set off to the dive site in the panga.

When we arrived and started to suit up, another diver noticed a broken clip on his fin, thus rendering it useless. There was just one other panga in the area waiting for its complement of divers to surface. We considered waiting for them so that we could borrow one of their fins. However, with a bit of ingenuity and lateral thinking, we managed to use the string from a drawstring bag to fashion a makeshift tie for the fin. That turned out to work quite well, and the dive was able to proceed after all.

The dive was quite nice, but there was nothing extraordinary. There was no coral around the dive location, but there were plenty of large pelagic species to be found. The bottom composition was a sandy seabed with lots of large boulders.

The highlight of the dive was a large, white-tipped reef shark circling us. At one point, the seabed also seemed to be alive, with garden eels poking their heads out of the sand.

Another diver, a young Welshman living in Brazil, and I were the first to reach our 50 bar (725 psi) threshold. We were, therefore, the first to surface after our three-minute, five-metre safety stop.

Once everyone was back aboard the panga, we returned to NEMO I for lunch. There was to be a second dive at the exact location, but I thought I'd seen what was to be seen there and decided to skip it. Two of the divers had only intended to dive once anyway. The second dive was cancelled since Juan Carlos did not want to dive with just one passenger.

Our second landing for the day was a wet one. It was a five-minute panga ride to a long, white, sandy beach for a few hours of free time. The beach was littered with sea lions lying on the sand or frolicking around.

There were plenty of other people from other boats walking up and down the shore, and it was a truly bizarre sight to see the sea lions and people mixing with a complete disregard for each other — apart from the fact that some of the humans were photographing some of the sea lions.

We spent much of our time on the beach just walking the length of it and back, trying to spot as many species of Darwin finches as we could.

Bird spotting was put on the back burner shortly before we were due to be collected again when one of our group members pointed out an enormous school of rays just a few metres from the shore. There must have been thousands of them swimming in close formation. From the shoreline, it looked like an eerie organic oil slick moving along the coastline. Even Juan Carlos was amazed at the size of the gathering.

As if that wasn't enough, several turtles were swimming close to the shore along with the rays. Now and then, one would poke its head out of the water and then hover beneath the surface. It almost seemed like they were checking to see if the beach was clear before coming ashore. They came ashore later in the evenings and at night. Unfortunately, all the uninhabited Galápagos Islands were off-limits from six o'clock onwards, so we would not see them on land.

Juan Carlos had brought a two-way radio with him. It was either not working, or nobody on the boat could hear the calls to come and collect us. Accordingly, we were the last group to leave the island. When the panga finally came to collect us, we spent a few minutes slowly following the huge schools of rays that had now split into several smaller groups. It was a truly fantastic sight.

The captain was evidently eager to set sail for our next destination. We noticed the NEMO I approaching to rendezvous with us. It was by now dusk. We had our briefing on what to expect from tomorrow. It was clear that there would be another early start for the divers. After dinner, I set up the laptop to run the now customary slideshow of our daily photos. Some four hundred snaps later, after a spontaneous round of applause, I wrote a few journal notes and went straight to bed. I was feeling a little off-weather and was exceedingly tired.

Day 402: Friday, 15th April, 2005, NEMO I

Today was a complete disaster for me. During the night, I'd developed a bit of a tummy bug and was up and down to the toilet every half hour. I was so lethargic and tired by morning, with aches and pains all over, that I could not even get out of bed. I spent almost the entire day resting in the cabin, trying to fight off whatever was ailing me. Sandy checked my temperature several times throughout the day. It continued to climb. It wasn't dangerously high, but at 38.4^0C (101^0F), it was enough for me to decide to start a regimen of Cipro antibiotics.

Naturally, I missed the diving and the day's island excursions. As it turned out, I wasn't the only one suffering; one other passenger and the captain had also succumbed to a tummy bug. We couldn't identify the source since those of us who had fallen ill had not eaten the same food.

Also, plenty of others who had eaten the same food were unaffected, so it was hard to say what could have caused the illness.

I was so tired throughout the day that I could barely leave the cabin to eat. All I could manage was an apple for lunch and a bowl of noodles for dinner.

The other ill passengers were recovering by the end of the day, but my fever hadn't broken by late afternoon. Sandy discussed that with

Juan Carlos. He decided to take me to a doctor when we reached Puerto Ayora, where we were heading.

One of the two catamaran's engines was experiencing problems. By the time we reached Puerto Ayora, it was with the aid of the main sails. The engine problem turned out to be a broken O-ring, which the ship's engineer was able to fix.

The other main news of the day was an apparent political uprising in Quito. We were concerned about our flights being affected by that turn of events. The whole thing turned out slightly more subdued than we were first led to believe. I suppose there's nothing like a good revolution now and then.

There was a decent recompression facility in Puerto Ayora on Santa Cruz. Juan Carlos took Sandy and me to see one of the two doctors there. We only had to wait about ten minutes before seeing the physician. Juan Carlos was able to translate between the Spanish-speaking chap and myself. His prognosis was mild dehydration with a possible stomach parasite. The recommendation was to continue with the Cipro regimen, which I'd already started, for the next four days and to take a one-time dosage of parasite-busting tablets.

According to the doctor, ninety per cent of people who pass through Ecuador and the Galápagos Islands, including many locals, would pick up the amoebic parasite. He said I could take Ibuprofen for the headache as needed. He also gave me a prescription for a stool sample analysis should I not start to feel better by tomorrow. The doctor's visit and the parasite tablets I bought from them at the facility's pharmacy set us back US $42 (€32.31), which we paid using our credit card.

Quite by coincidence, we bumped into Alyson and Albert, the same couple we spent the day with in Quito at the dock. They had arrived for their Galápagos Islands cruise. Sadly, we had just enough time to say hello and goodbye again on our way to the doctor.

We also saw one of the Canadian couples with whom we had dined in Puerto Ayora before the start of the cruise. They passed us by in a water taxi. It seems we were constantly bumping into people we'd previously met.

We lent Juan Carlos some cash that evening. I didn't bother to ask what the circumstances were. He was going out of his way to take care of me, and it would probably just come out of his tip anyway, so things would work out in the end.

We stopped at the supermarket on our way back from the doctor's appointment to pick up a few bottles of Gatorade. The doctor wanted me to drink a bottle of water and then a bottle of Gatorade alternately throughout the day. That was the best way to prevent dehydration. I also took the opportunity to stock up on chocolate — after all, I did need my energy.

The crew on the NEMO I were brilliant. None spoke much English, but the cook was concerned he might somehow be responsible for the apparent outbreak of illness aboard. We couldn't isolate a single food source common to the three affected people, so we weren't convinced there was a commonality.

I also later learnt the captain had suggested that Juan Carlos remain on board for the evening since a couple of people were not feeling too well. Several of those small clues had revealed just how well the crew had been looking out for the best interests of its passengers.

We'd missed dinner by the time we returned to the boat, but I wasn't feeling like eating much anyway. I ate an apple to help me take my two huge parasite tablets and went straight to bed following Juan Carlos' briefing for tomorrow.

Day 403: Saturday, 16th April, 2005, NEMO I

I was feeling much better this morning. Between the Amoeba parasite tablets and the Cipro, I was thankfully getting on top of whatever the problem was. I still had some diarrhoea, but I could at least eat a bit and participate in the day's activities. I even ate some breakfast of fried eggs, bread, and fruit juice. There was also some sort of frankfurter and vegetable mix, but I didn't fancy the look of it.

We discussed the possibility of everyone eating out that evening, but there wasn't a lot of enthusiasm for it. Sandy and I craved a fresh rotisserie chicken, so we wanted to explore that option later. The cook would be making chips for dinner, so that'll also be something to look forward to.

The NEMO I was just one of a small handful of cruise boats docked at Puerto Ayora that morning. It was perhaps fortunate that we could not secure a guide for that trip into the highlands just before we started the cruise a few days ago. It turned out that the tour was included in our itinerary after all. It would be the first part of today's activities.

The panga ferried us all the short distance to the now very busy and bustling Puerto Ayora dock. Fortunately, a refreshingly air-conditioned bus was already waiting for us. We sat in blissful comfort as we made our way inland. Juan Carlos gave us a running commentary on the different vegetation zones and pointed out the continuing changes in the landscape.

A half-hour later, we were let out at the site of some vast sinkholes. There were a couple of them, each cylindrical and about 100 m (330 feet) deep and about twice that in diameter.

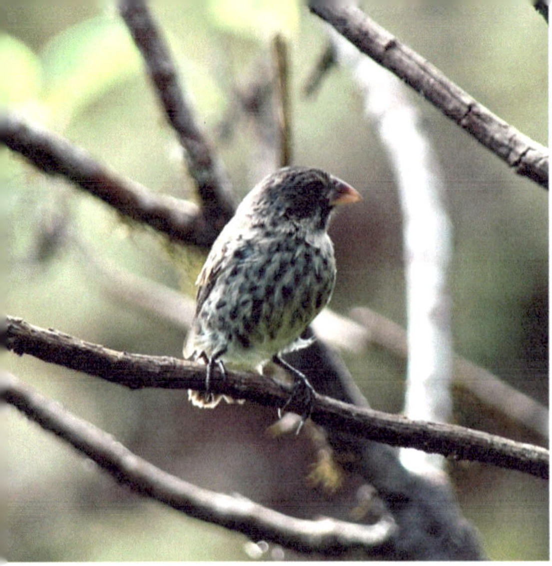

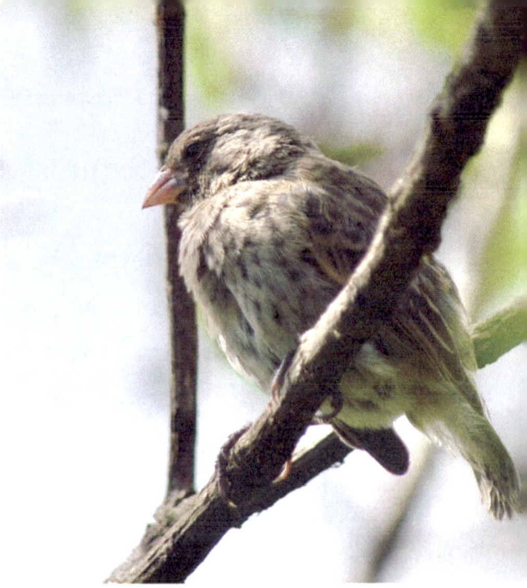

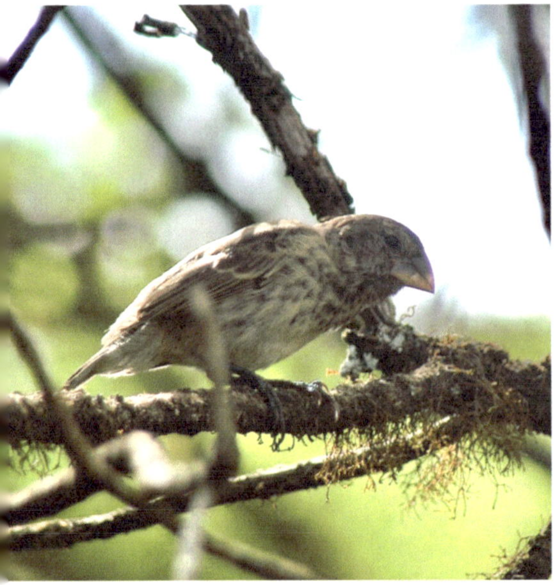

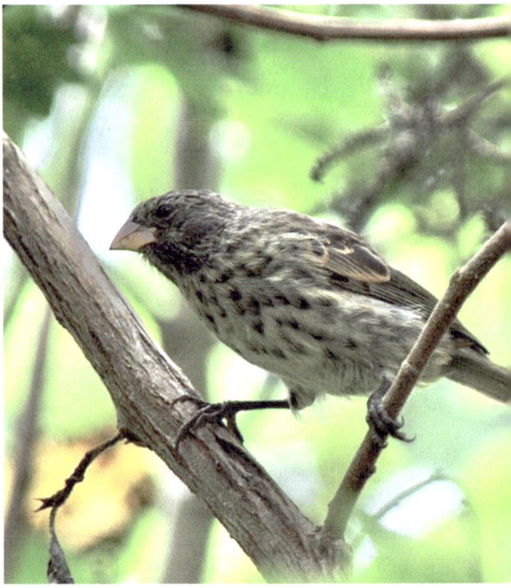

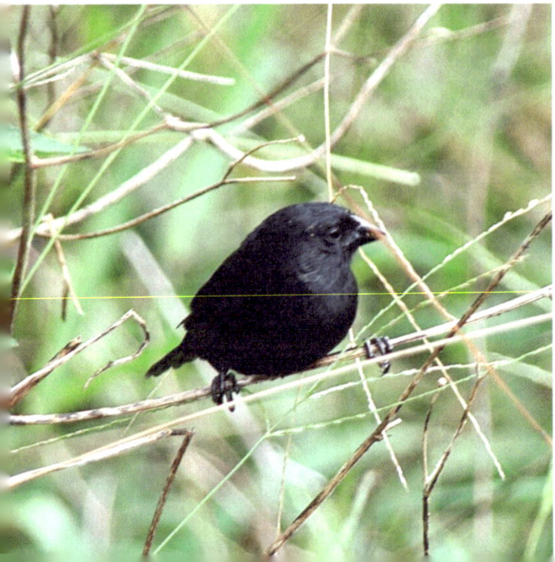

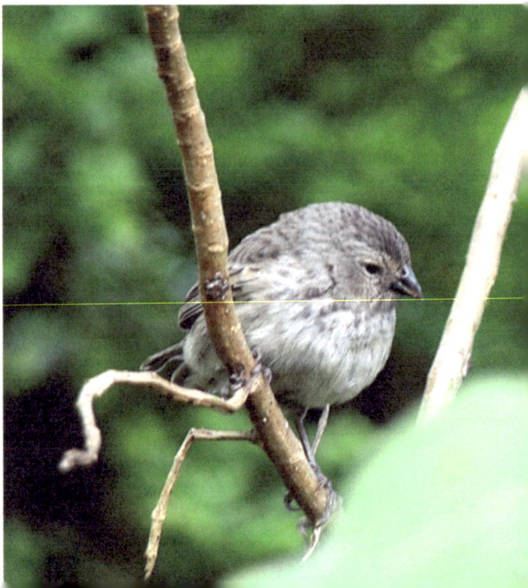

The sinkholes were impressive, but we spent most of the time trying to get some good shots of the large numbers of Darwin finches flying around. There are a dozen or more species around the Galápagos Islands. I'd been trying to get a good shot of as many of them as possible. As we walked from one sinkhole to the next, the whole single-file row of us stopped to get a closer look at one finch perched in the branches just ahead.

In every group, one always stands out by not following the rules. We had one such person in our group, too. He brazenly walked down the line and straight through the path ahead of us, thus scaring away all the birds, including the one we were gingerly trying to approach.

He was blissfully unaware of the damage he had just caused and seemed to somehow thrive on going against the grain and not following the rules, such as sticking with the group.

Juan Carlos was so upset that we all doubled back and got back on the bus again. We had to wait for our misfit to realise he was alone and return to the bus before continuing our highlands tour.

The real reason we went into the highlands was not the geology but the giant Galápagos tortoises that roamed around there. Like the wildebeest of the Serengeti, those unlikely-looking giants spend nearly the entire year on the move. They spent about six months migrating towards the lowlands in search of water and then another six months towards the higher ground again. Even though they were enormous and very slow, we still, unbelievably, had to take a tracker with us to assist in finding them.

He quickly found a male and a female sitting blissfully in the middle of a small swamp up to their necks in water and thick mud.

During last night's briefing, Juan Carlos had already told us about the different species and how to recognise them. We walked around for nearly an hour, trying to find as many as possible. Ultimately, we managed to find an additional three loners following the first two. None of those subsequent finds were sitting in water, so we got some very nice close-up photos.

As we moved through the thick vegetation, Juan Carlos plucked a few fruits from the various trees, and we tried some of them. I thought they were passion fruits. They were round and about the size of a lemon, with many jelly-covered pips inside that had a distinct flavour. They were delicious but had a very sharp and intense taste indeed.

There was a shack with a bar and toilet facilities at the end of our tortoise trek, so we could sit and enjoy some refreshments for about half an hour — not on the toilets, of course.

The Darwin finches were fluttering about in great numbers again, but what kept us most amused was Juan Carlos trying to ride one of the nearby horses. He galloped up and down for a while on one of them bareback but later learned that it was completely wild.

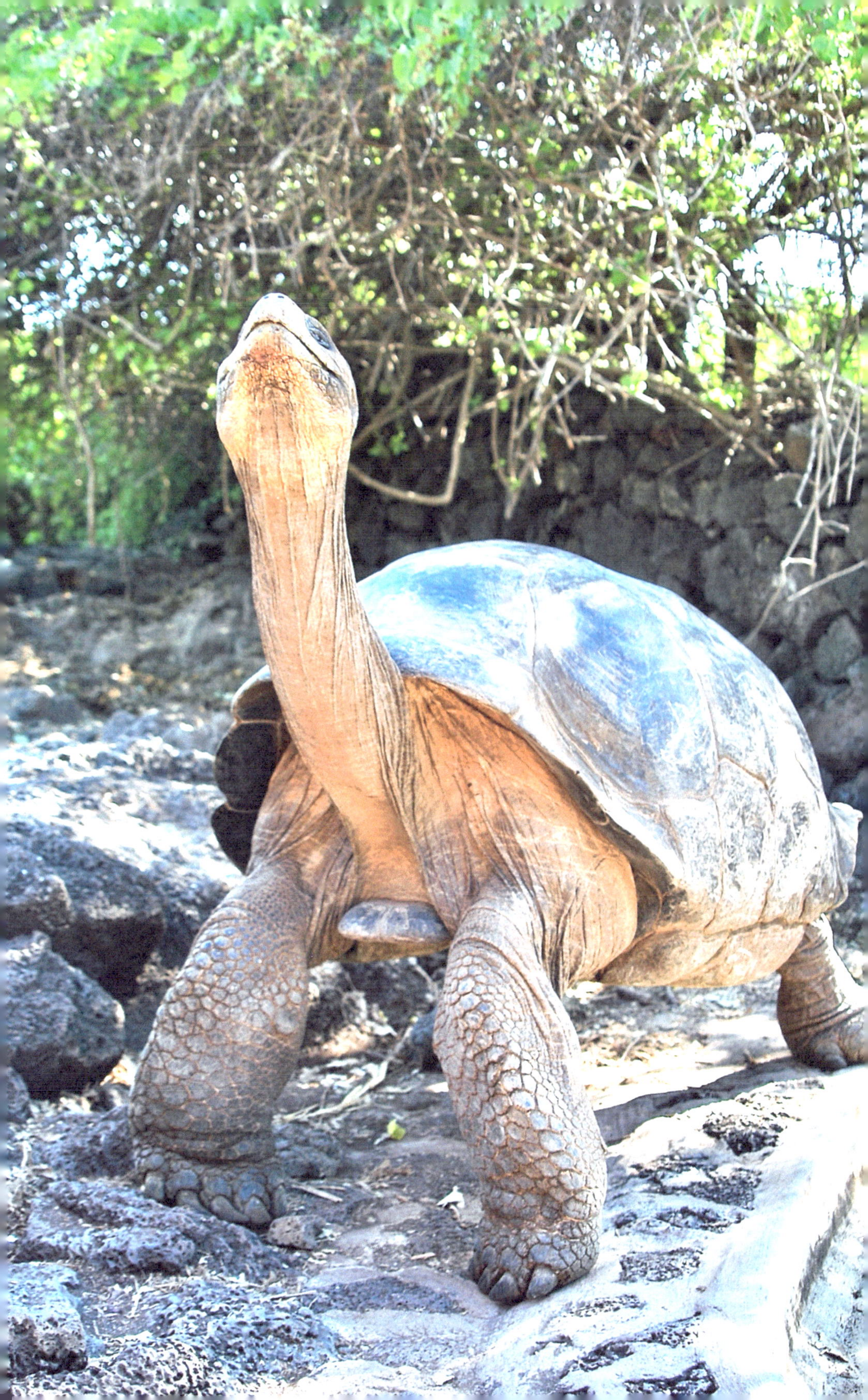

We went to see one other geological feature in the highlands. That turned out to be a rather large lava tube. That was quite a sizeable one as they went, and we could have driven a bus through.

It was a good couple of hundred metres in length. Those tunnels in the earth were formed by molten lava flowing through them during past geological activities. We'd seen them before, but nowhere near as large as this one.

Juan Carlos did his best to sing over the coach's intercom system, providing entertainment for our half-hour ride back into town. He did his best to get everyone to try to sing something. About half the group was brave enough to give it a bash.

Back aboard NEMO I, lunch was served. Everybody could rest for an hour to recover from the day's excursions. I took the opportunity to catch up on some backlogged journal writing.

Juan Carlos took the panga into town to run a couple of errands, and I gave him a bag full of our laundry to take with him to drop off and get cleaned.

Our second excursion for the day was to the Charles Darwin Research Institute. That facility was operated in cooperation with the Galápagos Islands National Park but was funded by grants from institutions such as UNESCO and the WWF. The national park got its funding from the park entrance fees, which every visitor to the archipelago had to pay upon arrival.

We had already visited the research station before the cruise started. However, we thought we'd learn more with our naturalist guide taking us around all the sites. Indeed, we did get to experience more this time compared to what we saw the previous time.

However, the place was teeming with visitors, with a couple of sizeable ships in port today. It was crowded to the point that it was less enjoyable. Still, we got to see all the giant tortoises again, including Lonesome George, the last remaining Pinta Island tortoise. He was discovered in 1971. Efforts had been underway to find a mate for him to prevent the extinction of his species.[4]

---

[4] The preservation of the Pinta Island tortoise species was unsuccessful. Lonesome George died in 2012. He was estimated to be around a hundred years old at the time of his death. His body was preserved and is now displayed at the American Museum of Natural History in New York City. Despite being the last of his kind, Lonesome George became a global icon for conservation efforts in the Galapagos Islands and around the world.

There was one book and souvenir shop within the research station grounds. The station received proceeds from every sale, so I picked up a Galápagos Islands wildlife identification book — after getting Juan Carlos to confirm it was the best book to buy.

I lent Juan Carlos some more money that afternoon. We thought the total of US $110 (€84.61) I'd now lent him would be a suitable tip for him. We'd now nearly exhausted our US dollar cash supply. We'd probably use some of our Pounds Sterling to tip for the captain and his crew.

After our guided walk around the facility, we were allowed another hour and a half of free time. As we'd already seen everything twice, Sandy and I returned to town to get a water taxi back to our boat. It was mid-afternoon, and we struggled to progress through the blistering heat. We had to sit down for a few minutes on the way there. Fortunately, we could flag down a taxi for the remainder of the journey.

I used my spare time aboard NEMO I to catch up on my backlogged journal entries. Those were the last few remaining entries I would commit to this journal. I could feel the urge to want to leave it at just writing up the notes, safe in the knowledge that I could complete everything once in Florida. Deep down, however, I knew it would be much better to get things down whilst everything was still fresh in my mind, so I kept telling myself to push ahead for that final stretch.

The panga arrived just as I finished the last journal entry. Juan Carlos joined me to head back into town to see about finding a rotisserie chicken for dinner. We'd seen at least a couple of places that sold them on the way back from our coach trip into the highlands. We were both very much looking forward to a decent meal of our favourite food that evening.

We found the place we had earlier seen, and plenty of fresh and already-cooked chickens were rotating on the spit outside the restaurant. They looked delicious, so I had the woman prepare a couple of birds to take back with us. She cut and wrapped them in foil for us and handed them over in a plastic bag. However, you could have knocked me down with a feather when she told us that they were US $15 (€11.54) each! At that point, my drooling lust for a fresh rotisserie chicken was more potent than my budget protection reflexes, so I reluctantly handed over the money. Ordinarily, I would have put up much more of a fight and might have tried to haggle for a while, but I wanted that chicken, and I wanted it now!

After collecting the ready and dried laundry, we wasted no time returning to the NEMO I. Unfortunately, the fact that Juan Carlos knew just about every man, woman and child living in Puerto Ayora meant he had to stop and chat with several dozen people along the way.

The chicken was still steaming hot when we made it back, though, and the regular ship's dinner was just about being served by the time we boarded. We managed to sit with the entire group anyway. Sandy, Juan Carlos, and I feasted on the succulent chicken.

I offered the last half portion of the bird to the captain, for which he seemed very grateful. We gorged ourselves and were utterly sated by the end of the meal.

It was a perfect ending to the day with another successful slideshow viewing of our day's photographic endeavours. We both hobbled into bed, absolutely stuffed.

Day 404: Sunday, 17th April, 2005, NEMO I

Once again, I was feeling better this morning compared to the previous, although still with a bit of diarrhoea. Just about everybody on the boat had diarrhoea during that voyage. Still, it could have been much worse. As a result, nobody lost more than half a day out of the packed itinerary. I would continue with the regimen of Cipro antibiotics until the entire five-day course was complete.

With all the early morning activities we'd been enjoying, everybody's internal clocks were slowly resetting themselves, as most people were up and about before the bell rang today. Juan Carlos was conspicuous by his absence. We soon learnt he was now the next in line to fall foul of what we were now thinking had been amoebic dysentery.

Our morning departure of exploration was delayed a couple of times as he tried to get himself together, but he could hardly stray more than a few inches from his cabin bathroom. I knew exactly how he felt. He did eventually show up but looked awful. We all felt sorry for the poor guy. We were also all wondering what would happen now that the only naturalist guide on the vessel was out of commission. The fact that he was the only one on the boat capable of communicating effectively with the crew was also a little disconcerting.

It was illegal for passengers to visit any islands without a naturalist guide, and Juan Carlos's illness could have ended the cruise for everybody.

We were due to visit the small island of Bartolome and climb up to the top of one of its volcano crater rims. That was now starting to look very much in jeopardy. Like the trouper he was, and much to everybody's surprise, our intrepid guide soldiered on and insisted we all get into the panga to ride to the island.

From the embarkation point, an elevated wooden walkway led around and up to the volcano peak. It was soon excruciatingly clear that Juan Carlos was in no fit state to climb anywhere. He barely managed to make it out of the panga. He made it a few steps with us but had to sit down from sheer exhaustion. Since there were no other boats at that visitor site and the path up to the top was clearly defined by the walkway, we all agreed he should stay put while the rest of us meandered up at our own pace. He bent the rules on that occasion quite reluctantly but with no energy to do otherwise.

It turned out to be quite an exhaustive climb up to the top. The island's landscape was nothing short of Martian. It was desolate, with almost no vegetation at all, and looked exactly like what I imagined a recently erupted volcano might have looked like several million years ago. It was as if the volcanic eruption had occurred recently, and the lava flows had only solidified yesterday. At just a couple of million years old, Bartolome is the youngest of the Galápagos Islands, a mere baby in geological terms. We could see almost no weathering of the sharp and jagged rocks that lay still since the lava first cooled. The entire landscape looked like it had been completely frozen in time.

We spotted the odd lava lizard scurrying around, but other than that, the only movement was the light wind gently blowing fine dust, which gave the whole place an eerie, desolate feel.

When we eventually made it that far up, the views from the crater rim were nothing short of mind-bogglingly spectacular. Directly ahead of us, we could see where two larger island masses were joined together by a concave strip of land between them. A pristine, golden sand beach straddled either side of this conjoining strip with some green vegetation in the middle. Those of us who made it to the summit first sat there in silence, watching the magnificent early morning scene. It was a truly magical experience, and I could think of nothing better to do at that moment.

There was, in fact, another boat that was moored at Bartolome. It was a much larger one that had already ferried several panga loads of visitors to the island and back. We had all been sitting on the NEMO I, cursing that such a large boat was in the area and flooding the visitor sites with boatloads of passengers. Nothing could spoil the scenery as quickly as a massive boatload of visitors flooding the area. They were by now visiting the other side of the island, snorkelling from one of the beaches on the slither of land that we could see from the top of the volcano.

We got close to a magnificent lava heron by the panga. It stood there oblivious to us and posing for the cameras. With the other much larger boat in the area, we convinced Juan Carlos to have the captain radio over to them. We wanted to see if they had any of the medication on board that was so successful in curing me of the same problem now afflicting him. The captain did so when we were all back safely aboard and went over there personally to collect it. He brought back enough medicine for both Juan Carlos as well as the other passenger on board, who had also succumbed.

Although we could barely communicate with our stout captain, he did his best to take good care of everyone onboard. I'd call that the sign of a very competent and professional captain. His presence exuded authority and compassion.

Since the second morning excursion was nothing more than the chance to snorkel from the beach, Juan Carlos retired to his cabin for some much-needed rest whilst we all donned our fins and masks to swim.

There had been an absolute wealth of things to see everywhere we'd snorkelled, at least on a par with what I might have expected to see SCUBA diving. Every island in the archipelago teemed with fish and marine life of all shapes and sizes right in the shallows close to shore.

Several penguins were flying around underwater at high speed chasing fish at this site, but I was, unfortunately, the only snorkeller not to see them — typical! I took my underwater camera with me and got some smashing photos, nevertheless.

Today was to be one of the days that diving was on the agenda, but with Juan Carlos clearly in no fit state to stand, much less get into his kit and go diving, it was starting to look very doubtful that we would get to submerge. Avrum, the only other diver passenger on board, suggested he and I go down alone, but the captain wouldn't allow it.

Just before he disappeared into his cabin, Juan Carlos told us that we would go diving since one of the crewmembers was a certified dive master. The captain sailed the NEMO I the hour or so over to the dive site. As soon as we arrived, he told Avrum and me we would not be allowed diving. He and Juan Carlos had miscommunicated with each other, and it transpired that the crewmember in question was not a dive master after all. The captain was extremely apologetic but insisted that there would be no diving without a competent dive master. I had no problems with that at all. Sure, it would be a shame to miss the opportunity to get into the water, but I wouldn't want to put my own life at risk to get that chance. We acquiesced to the captain's wishes on that one.

Just as we were starting to sail away from the dive site, someone spotted the unmistakable shape of a couple of fins sticking out of the water. That shark was about 15 m (50 feet) off our starboard side. The captain told me he thought it might have been a Galápagos shark. It got everybody's blood pumping. I would have liked to have gotten close to it under the water. Oh well.

With some free time to suddenly kill, everybody just chilled out around the boat. I took the opportunity to catch up on some very backlogged journal writing.

Sandy mentioned she was starting to feel queasy. I worried she might be the next to fall. Fortunately, it was little more than a mild bout of seasickness.

I wouldn't call three out of fourteen people on board falling ill an epidemic, but it did seem likely that something on the boat might be causing the illnesses. NEMO I had desalination equipment onboard to generate fresh water for the showers and so on. There was fresh drinking water on board from a water dispenser, but people showering and brushing their teeth with the desalinated water was one potential source of the problem. We'd probably never find out.

With the aid of the main sails, we reached our afternoon destination around the island of Santiago. That was another volcanic island. It had a jet-black ash sand beach, unlike anything I'd seen before. The black sand was remarkably striking, making for a rather odd-looking beach.

Several other small boatloads of visitors were already there enjoying themselves, either sitting on the beach or snorkelling. Having taken his anti-parasite tablets, Juan Carlos felt better when we reached that unlikely-looking beach. He disembarked with us to explore a short circuit around the landscape. He still wasn't talking as much, but he provided us with at least an abbreviated running commentary.

It had become clear that wildlife was the central theme for the first half of the cruise, which we had now moved on from. We were now exploring more landscapes and geology than anything else. It was no less fascinating. Every visitor site we explored was diverse.

Each was radically different to the last. It amazed me how there could be so much geological diversity within the confines of a single island group. Where we were on the island of Santiago, it looked like the lava had just stopped flowing yesterday. It was utterly pristine outside of the staked walkways.

We walked slowly around the circuit and marvelled at the surroundings. Juan Carlos's illness had something to do with our slower-than-normal progress, but with the sun beating down so intensely, none of us would have been able to move any faster, even if we wanted to.

When the lava flows started to solidify millions of years ago, they buckled and formed small arches. Under those arches, the effects of coastal erosion allowed the tides to come through and create crevices and blowholes. We walked gingerly over those natural bridges. All the cracks and crevices made them appear on the verge of collapsing.

In reality, the entire landscape had probably not changed over the past several thousand years or more. We expected to see marine iguanas everywhere but couldn't initially find any. As we moved around the rocky coastal area, someone spotted a massive gathering of probably upwards of a hundred or more huddled together.

After noticing that initial huddle, we looked around more closely and found several such groupings of the prehistoric-looking beasts.

Dotted around the black lava rocks teeming with iguanas were dozens of the now very familiar and beautifully colourful sally lightfoot crabs. Their brilliantly striking yellow, red and speckled blue shells were contrasted beautifully against the jet-black lava rock — so much so that we had to wonder what the evolutionary necessity must have been that drove such brilliant colouration.

By and large, the animals in the Galápagos Islands were fearless because they had evolved without any natural predators to worry about. We'd seen both herons and sea lions eating the crabs, so that was at least two natural predators for them, yet they were by far the most apparent creatures visible.

We saw plenty of the little lava lizards scurrying around. They were mostly slightly further inland, where the salty moisture from the crashing waves didn't reach. Juan Carlos happened upon a tiny scorpion and laid it down near a female lava lizard. She noticed the scorpion and pounced on it in a flash, devouring it. The lava lizards and the larger scorpions often went at each other with varying outcomes as to who was the victor.

Another unique feature of this island was the broken and dried coral all over the coastal areas. There were no coral reefs in the Galápagos Islands to speak of, at least nothing like the Red Sea in Egypt or Thailand, so it was a bit of a mystery as to why there was so much dead coral everywhere. One theory Juan Carlos was telling us about was that there might have been a coral reef when some of the volcanoes erupted millions of years ago. The broken pieces of white coral we could see everywhere might have been the remnants of the disruption to the reef in the past from those eruptions.

As we walked around the coast, all the ornithologists among us were thrilled to see several species of heron, oystercatchers, and other wading and seabirds. We also saw a few species we'd not yet seen, which always got our blood pumping.

The panga arrived to take us back to the NEMO I, where dinner was followed by the customary slideshow of the day's photos and the briefing for tomorrow's activities. Fortunately, Juan Carlos was now on the mend and feeling much better.

Day 405: Monday, 18th April, 2005, NEMO I

Once again, everyone was up bright and early that morning. That phenomenon of a slowly adjusting internal body clock was something we'd seen before during our overland safari tour through Africa. In the Galápagos islands, too, I found myself getting up earlier and earlier each day. In the rat race world, my ideal day would be ordinarily twenty-five hours long (or perhaps even longer) so I wouldn't have to contend with the daily gruel of waking up on the way to work. However, throughout our travels, I'd been quite happy to get up very early in the morning. It wouldn't last until we returned the grudge of the non-travelling lifestyle.

It was quite a shock for me when I climbed the ladder and peered through the hatch of our cabin that morning. The captain had moored us close to a vast sheer cliff face made from what looked like reddish-brown coloured layers of sediment. The entire island of Rabida was a brilliant reddish-tan colour. Juan Carlos explained it was due to ferrous oxide in the soil and rock. It was a bizarre sight. Yet again, we were surprised at just how amazingly different one island looked compared to the previous. It had been just one surprise after the other. The Galápagos Islands were a true geologist's dream come true.

Almost straight away, we noticed turtles in the water around us. They tended to sit at the surface for a while and pop their heads out to either look around or breathe now and then. After a few minutes of that, they usually submerged again. There were plenty of turtles around the islands. We kept seeing them everywhere we went.

The cook prepared some omelette for breakfast. He threw in several bits of who knew what, and I didn't fancy the look of it. I sufficed with a couple of pieces of the obligatory sliced fruit that was also laid out.

Juan Carlos noticed my expression when I looked at the omelette surprise without me realising it. He reminded the cook to note the various things that Sandy and I didn't eat and to keep this in mind when preparing meals. Before I knew what was happening, the cook handed me a separate plate with fried eggs. That was a nice touch, and it was gratifying to realise someone paid attention to such details.

Despite incorrect expectations getting me off to a bad start with our cruise, I was enjoying all the personal attention and care we were all getting. We had a butler, for want of a better word, on board. He tended to the cabins and served our meals. Food was often laid out buffet style inside the main cabin. The outside tables were nicely laid out with a tablecloth and cloth napkins. The butler laid out cutlery, glasses, and water jugs and collected all the plates and things when we were done with them. We didn't have to do very much other than eat the food presented to us.

Our first landing of the day was a wet one onto the tan-coloured sandy beach. With the wet landings, the panga was reversed towards the beach. Everyone then jumped out into knee-deep water. We'd now seen pristine beaches that had been white, golden-yellow, jet-black and now red — truly amazing.

Everyone immediately followed in single file for the most part (another example of conditioning) as we made our way around the staked circuit of this visitor site. As had become the case lately, the scenery and geology were the draw. We saw little wildlife, save for the odd lava lizard, a few birds here and there, and the Galápagos Sea Lions.

It was a short walk this morning, but we'd all brought our snorkelling gear with us on the panga. Most of the group remained to snorkel right from the beach whilst the divers among us took the panga back to NEMO I to prepare for that morning's dive.

Sandy told me to service the underwater camera equipment last night. I cheekily let her believe I did so, but the truth was that I was too tired. I figured I'd have time to do so this morning, so I rushed through the process of removing and re-greasing the O-rings and so on.

The NEMO I was a cruise vessel with optional diving instead of a diving cruise vessel. That may sound like a weak distinction, but there were some key differences. For example, there wasn't a dedicated dunk tank on board. There were, however, a couple of bins used to store shoes (shoes were not allowed to be worn onboard except on the diving platform), and Juan Carlos had emptied one of those to fill with water. I had asked him to do that since I needed a dunk tank to check for leaks in the underwater camera and strobe housings before each dive.

That morning, the makeshift dunk tank was once again filled with shoes instead of water — the crew were not used to the bin being filled with water, which would have been my guess as to why that was the case. With no functional dunk tank, the only way I could check for leaks was to step down onto one of the ends of the catamaran hulls to dip the camera into the salt water. I did that and couldn't see any leaks, so I took it for granted the camera was safely and correctly enclosed. It was hard to be sure due to the swells.

After kitting up and setting off in the panga, however, I noticed some fogging on the inside of the camera housing lens. Upon further inspection, I spotted a few drops of water inside. The housing was not watertight for some reason, and I had to leave the whole rig on the panga throughout the dive. I had already delayed the dive once by taking time to service the camera equipment. I didn't want to set everyone back even further by returning to see what the problem with the camera housing was.

I was not particularly impressed with the dive from the other day. Since I didn't have a camera with me, naturally, the dive was considerably better. I would have had a photographic field day had I had the camera with me. I couldn't believe my luck. Not only did we practically descend onto an adult, white-tipped reef shark, but we were also encircled by a group of amber jack right from the outset. To make matters worse, we followed a massive turtle and even stumbled onto a very rare and colourful Galápagos tiger eel snake.

I was pleased to have seen so many fantastic things during the dive but gutted not to bring any photographic proof back to the surface. Some people could travel the globe without a camera and still enjoy themselves. I'm completely the opposite. I often thought it a waste of time to go somewhere or see something if I couldn't take decent photos to record the event. I told Sandy about the mishap with the camera partially flooding. She was none too pleased about it either. Naturally, it was all my fault.

The missed photographic opportunity during the dive played on my mind for the rest of the afternoon. However, my attention was diverted when we reached our next destination about an hour later.

The Galápagos archipelago is a national park. The local fishing industry could practice its trade for the sole benefit of feeding the local population. There were, however, stringent rules and regulations. Even so, some local fishermen were known to disregard those rules. Shark fins, for example, fetched top dollar for the Asian markets. Fishing for sharks was still something that occurred around the Galapagos islands, albeit underground, so to speak.

Juan Carlos was usually emphatic about everybody sticking to the rules for the benefit of the protection of the pristine ecosystem. He became quite agitated when he spotted a small fishing vessel he thought was up to no good. He was not pleased at all.

He went over to talk to the fishermen about the infraction of setting foot on one of the small nearby islands. I didn't understand the Spanish, but the fisherman looked quite nervous and even a bit humbled by the admonishment he received.

I made doubly sure the camera housing was watertight for the second dive of the day. Even though it had its moments, it was not the spectacular dive that we experienced earlier that morning. I managed to collect just a small handful of decent shots.

With our photography both above and below the surface of the water being as prolific as it was and the fact that we continued to improve, it took a lot of work to satisfy our appetite for genuinely great photos. As our library of impressive photos grew, so did the difficulty in finding those shots that trumped the previous ones.

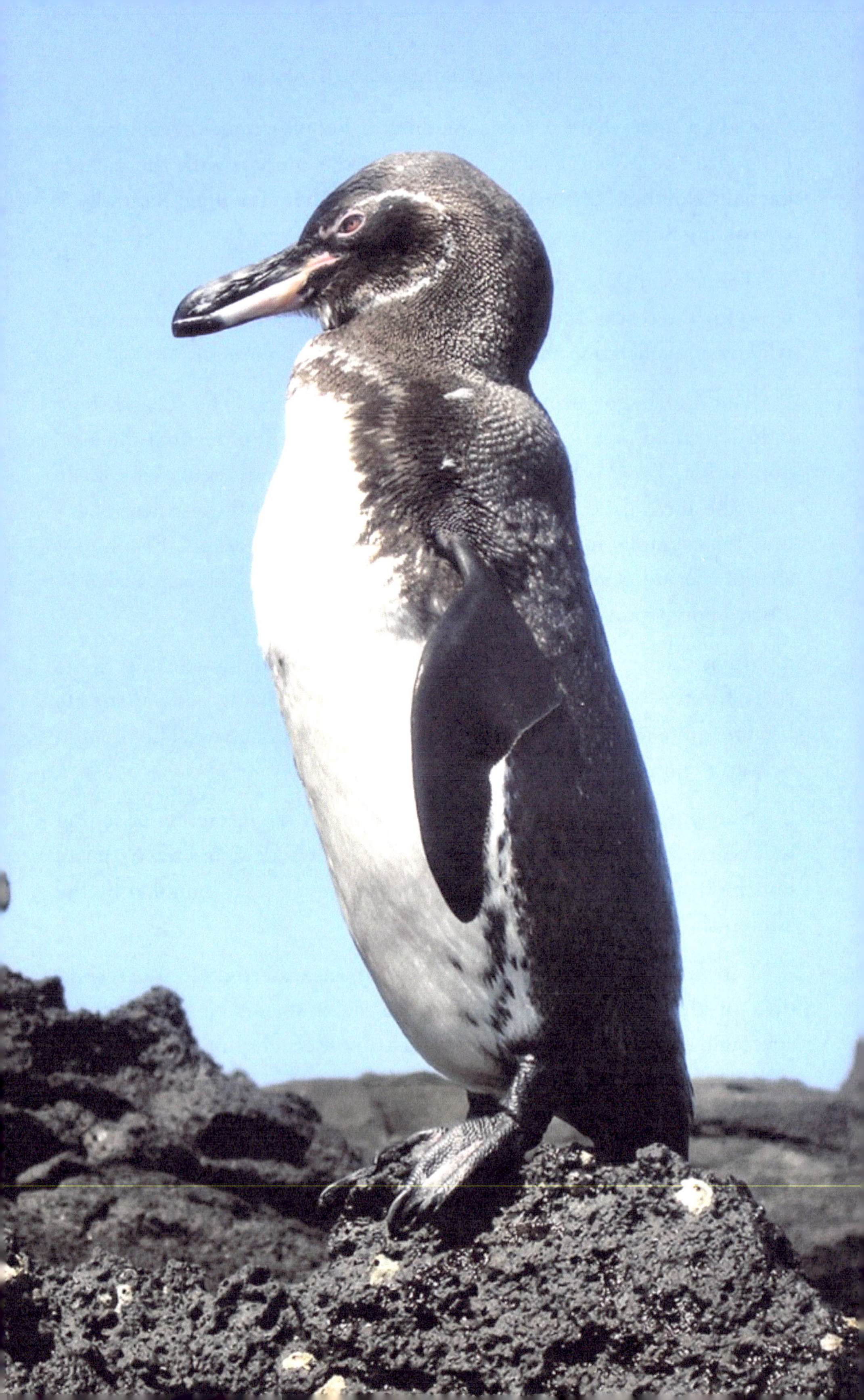

We did see another white-tipped shark (they were everywhere around those waters), and we swam through a couple of very impressive canyons, as well as seeing some very nice macro subjects, but the visibility was not terribly impressive and the debris in the water reflected from the strobe at times.

Following the completion of the dive, we were all allowed to snorkel in the immediate vicinity, but I had a problem just as I stepped off the panga. The valve in my snorkel tended to get stuck from time to time. I ended up sucking up nothing but water, so I had to motion for the panga to come and collect me again whilst I tried to remedy the problem. Fortunately, I was able to rectify the situation, so I carried on with my snorkelling.

Under the water was the usual array of spectacular marine life, but the real treat for us was a Galápagos penguin sitting on the jagged lava rocks right next to the water's edge. It sat there drying off and pruning itself. I managed to snorkel to within a metre of the beautiful bird to get some nice close-ups. We'd been looking for penguins for the past couple of days. This sighting was a real treat for everyone — especially me since most others had seen one while snorkelling yesterday.

The penguin was great, but the water's murkiness put a damper on any decent photography beneath the surface. As we climbed back into the panga, the realisation suddenly set in that this was the very last water excursion of the trip.

We made another wet landing later in the day. Walking around the lava flows and admiring the island's stunning geology was supremely enjoyable. That was concluded with a brief panga ride around to a spot where Juan Carlos found a grouping of four Galápagos penguins. We managed to get very close to those birds, too.

As we were all pointing our cameras, one of them decided to gingerly dive into the water and immediately fly around in search of small fish. The Galápagos penguin is the second smallest penguin, next to the blue penguin of New Zealand. With the top quarter of the archipelago above the equator, it was also the only penguin found in the northern hemisphere.

Back aboard the NEMO I, Juan Carlos was pouting over the fact that he had lent out a couple of decent Galápagos wildlife books to another boat. Those had been personally autographed to him by the respective authors. The guide on the other ship claimed that some passengers had taken the books on an earlier cruise. He was clearly very upset by this, and we all felt for him. Juan Carlos was quite a character. He had slowly become more than just our naturalist throughout the cruise. Everyone would miss him at the end of it all.

On the first day we arrived on the NEMO I, the owner was aboard for the afternoon. She was very impressed with a photo that I had taken of the vessel from the top of the mast when I was winched up there. I had promised to let her have that photo on CD, so I thought it might be nice to take some shots of the crew all standing next to the main sail with the name NEMO I on the sail visible in the background. I had all the crew assemble in their uniforms for an impromptu photo shoot and got some very nice shots in the process.

I spent much of the afternoon on a photographic hunt for the best shots and took some time to sort them all out on the laptop. I'd decided to sort out some of the best pictures from the overall cruise to give to the owner, along with the shots of the catamaran. That may just curry some favour regarding a possible return trip to the Galápagos Islands at some point in the future. I would love to return for a diving trip around some of the islands at the top end of the archipelago. Darwin and Wolf were the islands that stood out as the best diving locations throughout the archipelago. I would dearly love to dive there.

With that evening being the last of the cruise, Juan Carlos and the entire crew were on hand for a farewell ceremony and cocktail. Everyone was in a joyous mood. Juan Carlos made a very rousing speech about how well the trip had gone and how well everybody got on with each other, given that we were all strangers to each other on day one. Apparently, even the crew had commented on this too. Everybody shared his sentiments. It was indeed a genuinely successful cruise that everybody enjoyed immensely. Some survey forms were handed out, and I did my best to reflect my true feelings — both the good and the bad. The dinner that evening was just about the best I'd had so far. I ate every morsel put in front of me — the first time that happened since we first set sail.

Although he didn't want to advertise the fact, Juan Carlos had arranged with the owner that Sandy and I would not have to pay the bar bill for all the soft drinks we'd drunk over the past week. That was apparently a measure of goodwill in return for receiving a copy of that one photo the owner took such a liking to at the beginning of it all. I hoped she was happy with the whole CD of photos I left her.

We still had tomorrow morning to go, but looking back over the past week, all the passengers had bonded well together. Everybody would leave the vessel with new friends. After dinner, we all exchanged contact details. I made some CDs full of photos for everybody who asked — which was just about everybody.

We all started the laborious process of packing away our things. Everyone left their tips in the envelopes provided in our cabins. I told Juan Carlos to keep the US $110 (€84.61) we lent him as his tip. I also put another £60 (€90) in the crew's envelope. We spent the remainder of the evening playing cards and getting progressively drunk. It was a fitting final evening.

Day 406: Tuesday, 19th April, 2005, Quito

With our outbound flight from the Galápagos Islands already scheduled for later that afternoon, that morning's brief panga ride would sadly mark the termination of our Galápagos Islands cruise. Many passengers were still exhausted from yesterday evening's festivities. The mood around the deck was sombre. It wasn't openly discussed, but it was clear everyone had a really great time onboard. Consequently, we were sorry to be bringing a fantastic odyssey to a close. I, for one, would have loved to have stayed for longer. I was already thinking about possibly returning. Up to this point in our travels, people often asked me which was my favourite country. I always told them that if I had to choose a single country to return to, it would be either South Africa or Tanzania — both for wildlife viewing. The next time I'm asked that question, having completed this Galápagos Islands cruise, it will be a three-horse race with the Galápagos Islands in the mix, too.

The panga ride this morning preceded breakfast. There was just a hint of a chill in the still morning air. Knowing full well that the clouds would clear and the mercury would rise, everyone was still exposing most of their skin.

Juan Carlos and one other crewmember went with us to explore the nearby Black Turtle Cove. It was an inland series of secluded waterways, channels, and lagoons where the banks were lined with endless rows of mangroves. Turtles, sharks, and a whole host of other marine-dwelling creatures frequented that area to mate, lay eggs or give birth. The mangrove roots that grew through the water and into the mud provided a haven for the young fish against predators. That nursery was a crucial feature of the overall ecosystem. It would cause drastic knock-on effects on the natural food chain if disturbed. Fishing and development there were strictly prohibited.

We saw several small schools of different kinds of rays, plenty of birds, lots of turtles popping their heads out of the water from time to time and even quite a few immature sharks.

We trundled slowly around the lagoons, looking for movement in the waters. At one point, we stumbled into a sleeping group of six small white-tipped sharks just 20 cm (8") beneath the surface of the water.

It was a successful morning's panga ride overall, and well worth the effort to get up early. Back aboard the NEMO I, we all finished off what packing we each had left to do and pottered around a bit. People exchanged contact details with each other, and just about everybody extended an invitation to just about everybody else to stay with them whenever the opportunity arose.

The captain had steered us back the short distance to where it all started at the dock in Baltra and moored up to refuel the vessel. Those sea lions we first saw lazing under the jetty were still there. What piqued my interest straight away was what looked like a flock of brown noddies in an apparent feeding frenzy just at the surface of the water. A school of larger fish chased a larger school of smaller fish, jumping at the surface, trying to escape. The smaller fish were thus being preyed upon from beneath and above the water's surface.

As we disembarked for the final time, everybody shook the captain's hand and thanked the entire crew again for their efforts. It had been a phenomenal cruise. Everybody was sad to be leaving the catamaran. For another couple and us, it was a doubly sad moment as the termination of this Galápagos Islands cruise also signified the termination of our overall trip.

Despite the sadness that we were leaving, everyone was in a jolly mood. There were laughs galore as Juan Carlos accompanied us to the airport. We were booked on the latter of the morning flights with TAME. He helped us at the ticket counter to see about changing to the earlier flight, which would give us more time in Quito to sort out our accommodation for the night.

It was mayhem at the airport. Juan Carlos did his best to ensure we were all well cared for. He summonsed one of the national park workers to check our bags before departure. Apparently, they chose a couple of bags at random from each departing group of people to perform an inspection. Neither of our backpacks was chosen, so we were free to go and change our flight tickets.

It was all a bit confusing initially, but after the check-in staff learned that Sandy was pregnant, they wanted confirmation of that fact. We had to dig in our daypacks for the obstetrician reports we had from the scan in Melbourne. Even after seeing that paperwork, they still weren't happy. They insisted Sandy be seen by a doctor who could confirm she could fly. We'd never encountered that anywhere else before. Each country had little eccentricities, so we just went with the flow.

A young female medic in a small building just behind the check-in desk was on hand to ask Sandy some routine questions and provide the travel certificate the airlines wanted. We had to pay US $10 (€7.70) for the privilege, but we'd at least be allowed to board the flight. The medic also suggested the certificate would be helpful when we left Quito just in case the airlines there made the same fuss. At the very least, we learnt that Sandy's blood pressure was acceptable. Given she had high blood pressure in the past, knowing it was apparently under control was reassuring.

The time finally came for us to pass through the departure hall. We said our final goodbyes to Juan Carlos and all the other passengers who were also departing that morning. The same couple who had just finished their overall trip were also going to be spending the night in Quito tonight. We agreed to meet each other for dinner at TGI Friday's for our last Latin America meal.

Our plane was quite full. There was a six-year-old little Spanish-speaking girl travelling on her own in the seat next to me. I did my best to amuse her throughout the flight, but verbal communication, at least, was difficult. She seemed to enjoy listening to Disney music through my headphones connected to my laptop.

We stopped briefly at Guayaquil to let a few passengers off and on before pushing into Quito. Just as soon as we landed, it became readily apparent we were once again at high altitude. We were both finding it hard work to suck oxygen from the very thin air.

It being the last night of the trip, Sandy wanted to splurge on a nice hotel, so she sat to wait for the luggage belt to start moving while I meandered over to the international arrival terminal. A couple of pleasant young ladies staffed an information booth there. I had chatted with them when we first arrived in Quito.

A plush-looking Sheraton hotel was just across the street from the TGI Friday's restaurant. I asked the ladies if they could call the hotel on my behalf. I spoke to a charming young woman at the hotel's reception desk and asked about a room. I told her that my wife was pregnant (which had often helped lately), and she offered me a nice room for US $100 (€76.92).

Sandy's instructions were to ignore the cost and go ahead and book a nice room. I guess my haggling and negotiation urges were too dominant now, as I immediately started to haggle with the girl. I knocked her down to US $80 (€61.54) and then finally her boss down to US $70 (€53.85). We'd still have to pay the twenty-two per cent tax, but I figured the savings would at least pay for our evening meal. Job done! As a bonus, they sent over a complimentary shuttle to collect us. I thought this Four Points Sheraton in Quito, which turned out to be a five-star hotel, was fitting for the last night of our trip.

The room was gorgeous — about as good as a hotel room could be. It even had an Internet connection that I could plug into the laptop. After flopping onto the bed, I spent some time doing some last little categorisation chores from our Galápagos Islands photo library. We managed to retain just under two thousand shots altogether.

We met the other couple at the restaurant later that evening and enjoyed a wonderful time exchanging travel anecdotes with each other. By the end of the plentiful meal, we were all sated and barely able to keep our eyes open. Sandy and I arrived back at the hotel exhausted — not just from today but also from travelling in general.

Day 407: Wednesday, 20th April, 2005, Flight to Miami

It was late evening. We'd just arrived in our former hometown of Jacksonville, Florida. Since we were there to visit with friends and former neighbours, we were technically no longer travelling. As such, I considered our epic round-the-world trip to have concluded. The one flight that remained ahead of us was the one that would take us home three weeks from now. In doing so, we would have completed our global circumnavigation and final leg of this amazing journey.

As far as the travelling itself was concerned, we were done. This epic exploration of new places and cultures had finally ended. This would be my last log entry. It felt surreal to be back in Jacksonville. It felt like just yesterday that we left this all behind to embark on our new lives as worldly travellers. In a sense, then, we'd already come full circle.

I should reflect on the trip overall. The problem was that there were now so many new memories to draw upon that I felt strangely disoriented. I was in a bewildering labyrinth of emotions and experiences I couldn't possibly begin to summarise. It was fair to say Sandy and I had enjoyed being travellers immensely. After more than seven solid months on the road, however, we had both recently started to feel like the time was fitting to complete the trip. We were ready for a break.

I could vividly remember the first night of this leg of the trip. It was at a small, nondescript hostel just a short distance from Heathrow Airport near London. We opened the door to that first hostel room and peeked inside to see what it was like. As we walked inside, we crossed the threshold not just into the room but also into the world of the independent traveller, and our journey began. We'd returned to this side of that threshold and would soon be hanging up our trusty backpacks, kit bags, travel clothes and accessories. It may have been some time before we were again exposed to new cultures, architecture, landscapes, sights, and sounds. We would miss that adrenaline rush keeping us going when our bodies were tired and jetlagged from the long journey to a new place.

Travelling had conditioned us to a certain extent. Now that we were back in a developed Western society again, I noticed the little things that differed between regular life and many of the places we'd travelled through. Silly little things like not having to use toilet paper sparingly for fear of clogging the ancient and inadequate sewage system, not having to deposit the toilet paper into a bin next to the toilet for the same reason, being able to open the hot water tap and finding hot water coming out, seeing road users observe the traffic signals and markings on the road, and sleeping in a comfortable bed with a warm duvet. The list was as endless as it was obscure.

I learned a lot on the trip. I never knew there were so many different cultures and peoples around the world. It just wasn't possible to understand another culture through books or any other form of media. I now realise that TV and film were just about the worst means of educating people about the world around us. The world wasn't anywhere near the dangerous sort of place that the news media portrays. For example, there had been several countries where I'd been genuinely apprehensive about visiting because of my limited and warped understanding of what to expect there. Without exception, every place I'd been to had shattered my preconception of what I thought it would be like. I'd also felt safe in every country we'd been to.

There's no doubt about it: travelling broadens the minds. Sandy and I gained an understanding and tolerance for cultures, other perspectives, and other societies. When we decided to pack up, sell the house, and go on the road, I was initially concerned about the gaps that would create in my CV. However, the skills we learned while travelling have been among the most beneficial that I've been able to list on my résumé. Intangible skills, like planning, dealing with adversity, thinking on my feet, finances, tolerance, negotiation skills, adaptability, confidence, self-awareness, cultural understanding, appreciation for the natural world, geographical awareness, and many more were all skills we've picked up or radically enhanced as a direct result of this trip.

We also met fun and engaging people along the way and have kept in touch with many of them. We now have a war chest of memories to dine out on for the rest of our lives. Perhaps the most important friendship of all is that of Sandy and me. We became closer. We lived in each other's pockets 24 hours a day for days and weeks on end. In everyday life, even the most devoted partners don't do that. One might go to work daily, while the other might be at home. There are always times that you are apart. That's less so the case when two people are travelling together. Sandy and I connected at a profound and emotionally intense level. Don't get me wrong, we argued with each other occasionally. On occasion, one of us had to engage a relief valve. But we were always there with each other — we were our own emotional support network in the absence of the familiar surroundings of friends and family to otherwise fall back on.

Perhaps the most enduring legacy of this trip is our firstborn son, Joey, conceived in Australia — hence the name.

Sandy and I moved back in with John and Lisa for a short while. I quickly found a contract doing IT work in London (one of the benefits of having transportable skills that were in demand). Joey was born a few weeks later, followed by a sister for Joey a year later. We lived in the UK for 4 years before the global financial crisis struck with a vengeance. Out of work and with few prospects in that turbulent IT labour climate, Sandy and I decided to move to Australia. We spent 9 years living there before relocating back to the Netherlands. That was about 5 years ago.

I reflected often on our travels. With so many memories, it was hard not to. Finally, I decided to commit those memories for posterity and created this series of Round The World Travel memoirs. We hope you enjoyed reading them. I certainly enjoyed writing them and reliving all those memories. Thank you for being with me on this journey.

Thank you for joining us on this incredible journey around Oceania & South America. We hope our adventures have brought you joy, inspiration, and a touch of wanderlust.

If you enjoyed the book, please consider taking a moment to share your thoughts. Your reviews mean the world to us and help other readers discover the magic within these pages.

Safe travels, and may your adventures be as captivating as the ones we've shared.

Warm regards,

Christopher & Sandy Morgan

PHOTO IDENTIFICATION

Page	Description
18	Tahiti from the water
19	Christmas tree worms (Spirobranchus giganteus).
20	Spotfin squirrelfish (Neoniphon sammara).
	Hawksbill turtle (Eretmochelys imbricata).
21	Papuan Toby (Canthigaster papua).
26	Standing Moai.
27	Ahu Tongariki.
28	Partially buried Moai.
29	Standing Moai.
30	Ahu Tongariki.
31	Ahu Ko Te Riku, near Hanga Roa.
	Boats at Hanga Roa harbour.
34	Sandy on the outer edge of Rano Raraku.
35	Sandy at the Rano Raraku quarry.
36	Panoramic view of Rano Raraku.
37	Ahu Akivi.
39	Standing Moai at Ahu Ko Te Riku at sunset.
	Ahu Vai Uri at sunset.
42	Navel of the World geode.
43	View from a high elevation on Easter Island
44	Ahu Nau Nau.
45	Panoramic view of Anakena beach.
48	Panoramic view of Rano Kau Volcano caldera.
49	Petroglyphs at Rano Kao.
	Petroglyphs at Rano Kao.
50	Ahu Vinapu.
52	Rapa Nui performer.
	Rapa Nui performers.
75	Sandy before the Mitad del Mundo monument at the equator in Ecuador.
89	Sandy with Galápagos Giant Tortoise (Chelonoidis niger).
90	Yellow Land Iguana (Conolophus subcristatus).
91	Galápagos Mockingbird (Mimus parvulus).

97	Blue-footed Booby (Sula nebouxii) diving frenzy.
98	Blue-footed Booby (Sula nebouxii) sitting on the water.
100	Nemo I catamaran cruise vessel.
101	White-sand beach near Baltra.
102	Sally Lightfoot Crab (Grapsus grapsus).
	American Oystercatcher (Haematopus bachmani).
103	Nemo I from atop the main mast.
104	North Seymour Galapagos sea lions (Zalophus wollebaeki).
105	Magnificent Frigatebird (Fregata magnificens).
	Blue-footed Booby (Sula nebouxii) brooding an egg.
106	Blue-footed Booby (Sula nebouxii) in mating courtship dance.
	Magnificent Frigatebird (Fregata magnificens).
107	Blue-footed Booby (Sula nebouxii) brooding an egg.
108	Magnificent Frigatebird (Fregata magnificens) chick.
109	Yellow Land Iguana (Conolophus subcristatus).
	Female Galápagos Lava Lizard (Microlophus albemarlensis).
110	Juvenile Galápagos Sea Lion (Zalophus wollebaeki).
	Galápagos Marine Iguana (Amblyrhynchus cristatus).
111	Swallow-tailed Gull (Creagrus furcatus).
	Yellow Warbler (Dendroica petechia).
115	Galápagos Marine Iguana (Amblyrhynchus cristatus) blue.
	Galápagos Marine Iguana (Amblyrhynchus cristatus) red pair.
116	Female Galápagos Lava Lizard (Microlophus albemarlensis).
	Galapagos Albatross (Phoebastria irrorata) in flight.
117	Galapagos Albatross (Phoebastria irrorata) sitting.
118	Pair of Nazca Boobies (Sula granti).
	Galápagos Marine Iguana (Amblyrhynchus cristatus) red.
119	Galápagos Hawk (Buteo galapagoensis).
121	Galápagos Garden Eel (Heteroconger klausewitzi).
	Female White-spotted Boxfish (Ostracion meleagris).
122	King Angelfish (Holacanthus passer).
	Mexican Hogfish (Bodianus diplotaenia).
123	Longspine Porcupinefish (Diodon hystrix).
	Sea lions on Española beach
124	Sea lions on Española beach.
125	School of rays.
	School of rays.

126 Galápagos Flycatcher (Myiarchus magnirostris).
127 Sally Lightfoot Crab (Grapsus grapsus).
     Male Galápagos Lava Lizard (Microlophus albemarlensis).
128 Ecuadorean hairy hermit crab (Coenobita compressa).
129 Galápagos finches (sub-species unclear).
131 Sinkhole on Santa Cruz.
132 Galápagos Finches (sub-species unclear).
134 Santa Cruz Island giant tortoises (Chelonoidis porteri) in mud.
135 Lonesome George, a male Pinta Island tortoise (Chelonoidis niger abingdonii).
136 Santa Cruz Island giant tortoise (Chelonoidis porteri).
137 Possibly a Galapagos Yellow Warbler (Dendroica petechia aureola).
138 Galapagos Yellow Warbler (Dendroica petechia aureola).
139 Lava Heron (Butorides sundevalli).
141 Climbing Bartholome island.
142 Pinnacle rock, Bartholome island.
143 Lava Heron (Butorides sundevalli).
     Bravo Clinid (Gobioclinus dendriticus).
144 Giant Hawkfish (Cirrhitus rivulatus).
145 Galapagos ringtail damselfish (Stegastes beebei).
146 American Oystercatcher (Haematopus bachmani).
147 Galápagos Marine Iguanas (Amblyrhynchus cristatus).
     Bartolome island landscape.
148 Bartolome island landscape.
149 Bartolome island landscape.
     Galápagos Marine Iguanas (Amblyrhynchus cristatus).
150 Sally Lightfoot Crab (Grapsus grapsus).
     Lava lizard eating a scorpion.
151 Broken pieces of coral littering the landscape.
     Yellow-crowned Night Heron (Nyctanassa violacea).
153 Galapagos Sea Lion (Zalophus wollebaeki) on Rabida beach.
155 Gray-tailed Tattler (Tringa virgata).
     Flatworm (Pseudoceros bajae).
156 Giant Moray Eel (Gymnothorax javanicus).
158 Galapagos Penguin (Spheniscus mendiculus).
159 Queen Conch (Strombus gigas).

163   Juvenile Sharks in Black Turtle Bay.
      Rays (species unclear) in Black Turtle Cove.
164   Spotted eagle rays (Aetobatus narinari) in Black Turtle Cove.
      Brown Noddy (Anous stolidus).

Other books by Christopher D. Morgan

Travel Memoirs

https://ChrisAndSandyMorgan.com/travel

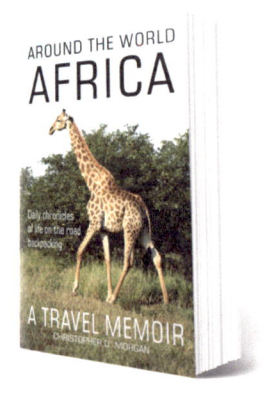

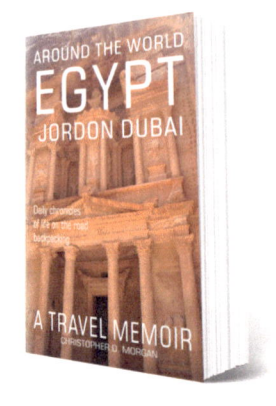

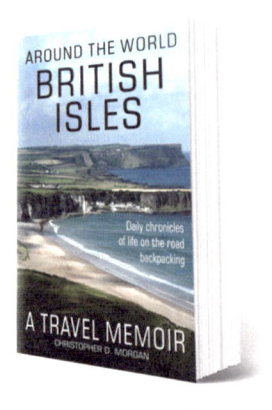

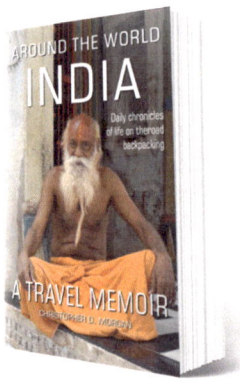

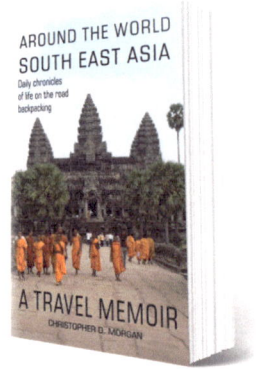

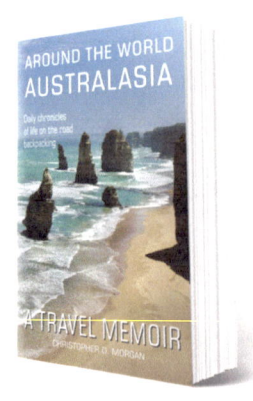

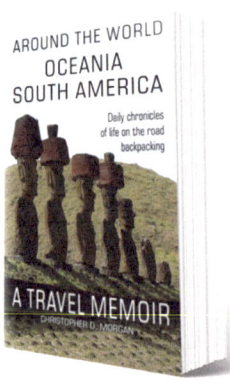

Embark on a captivating global journey with
AROUND THE WORLD: A 400 day photographic memoir.

This unique memoir encapsulates the essence of our 400-day expedition across continents, offering vivid recollections and stunning photo collages from each country visited.

Join us as we traverse diverse landscapes, delve into rich cultures, and share unforgettable moments from our epic adventure.

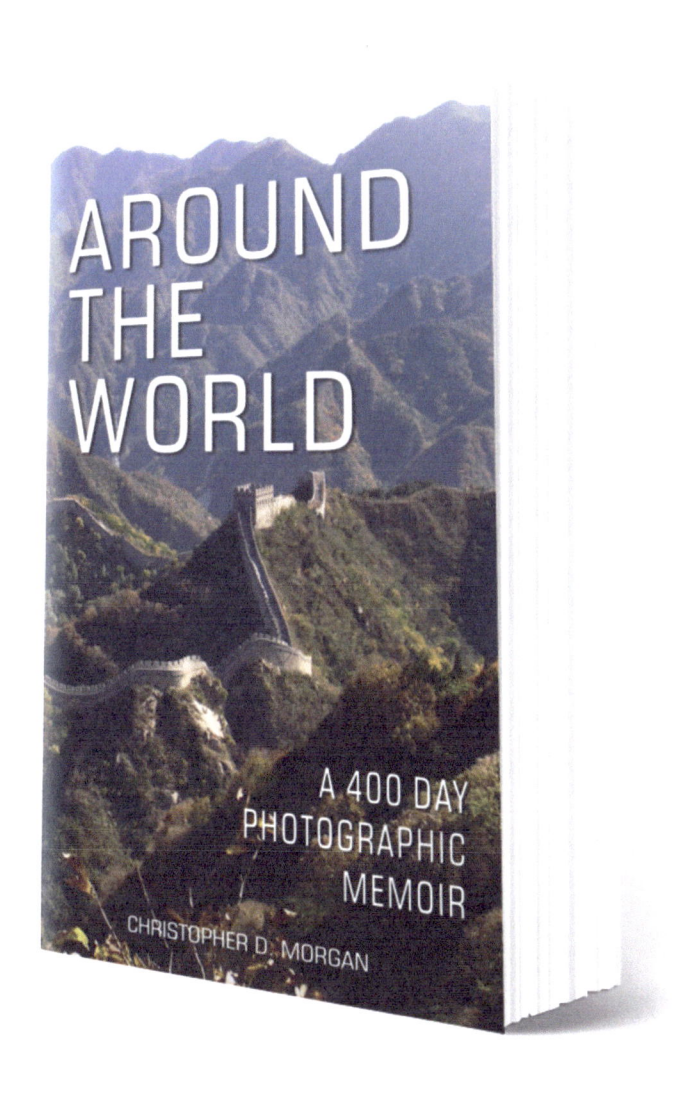

Fantasy Adventure Series

Dive into a different fantasy world in each book.

https://Portallas.com

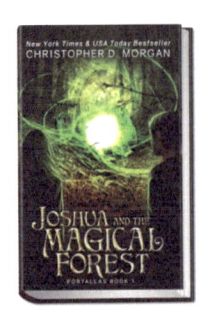

Joshua and the Magical Forest
Portallas book 1

Joshua and the Magical Islands
Portallas book 2

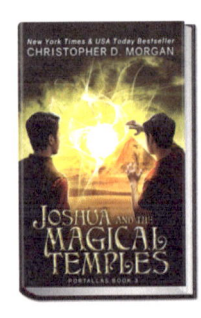

Joshua and the Magical Temples
Portallas book 3

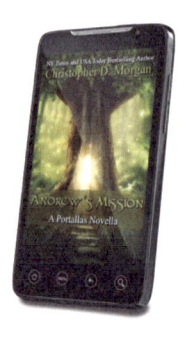

Andrew's Mission
A Portallas short story

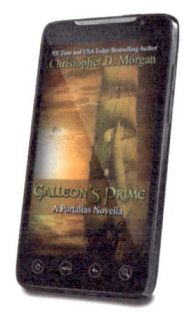

Galleon's Prime
A Portallas short story

Sarah's Farewell
A Portallas short story

Portallas: Adult Colouring Book

Portallas: Big book of Activities

Puzzle & Activity Books

Word puzzles, number puzzles, logic puzzles, puzzles for kids, teens, adults, therapy puzzles and many more.

Over 120 puzzle books in the collection and counting.
Below is a small selection.

https://BounceLearningKids.com.books

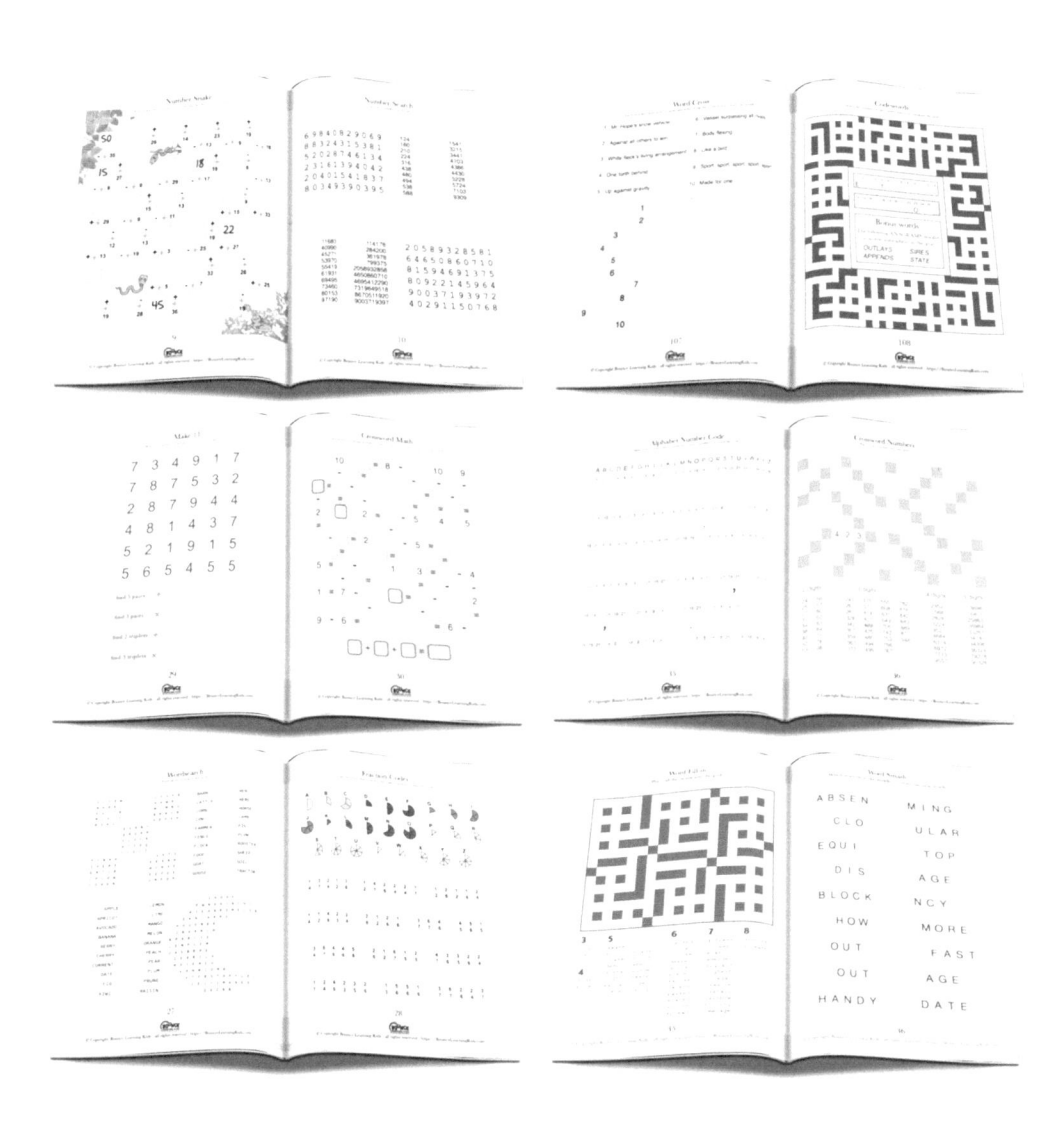

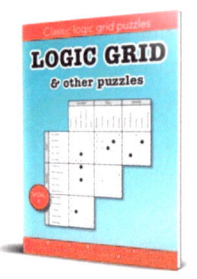

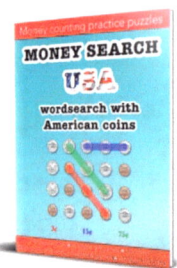

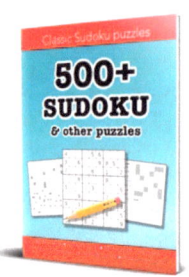

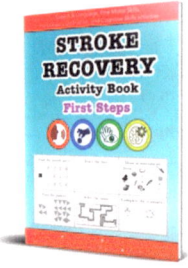

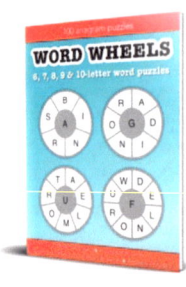

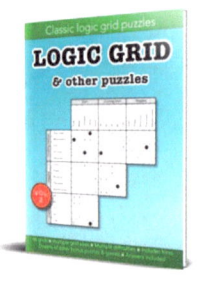

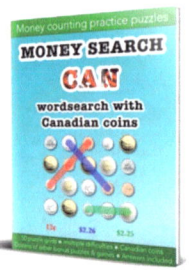

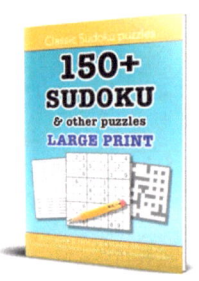

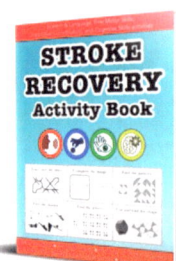

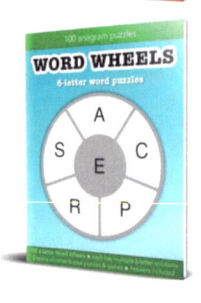

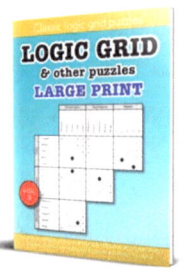

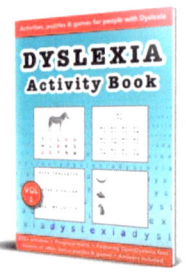

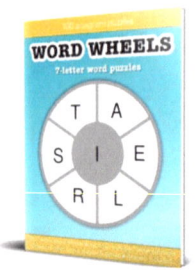

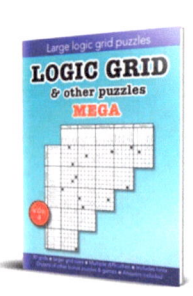

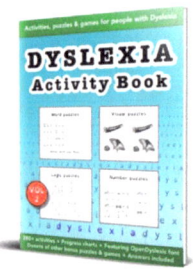

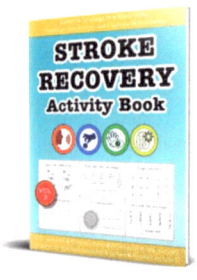

Logic Grid & other puzzles

- **LOGIC GRID** & other puzzles
- **LOGIC GRID** & other puzzles
- **LOGIC GRID** & other puzzles — LARGE PRINT
- **LOGIC GRID** & other puzzles — MEGA

Money Search

- **MONEY SEARCH USA** — wordsearch with American coins
- **MONEY SEARCH CAN** — wordsearch with Canadian coins
- **MONEY SEARCH UK** — wordsearch with British coins
- **MONEY SEARCH AU** — wordsearch with Australian coins

Sudoku & Dyslexia

- **500+ SUDOKU** & other puzzles
- **150+ SUDOKU** & other puzzles — LARGE PRINT
- **DYSLEXIA Activity Book**
- **DYSLEXIA Activity Book**

Stroke Recovery

- **STROKE RECOVERY Activity Book** — First Steps
- **STROKE RECOVERY Activity Book**
- **STROKE RECOVERY Activity Book**
- **STROKE RECOVERY Activity Book**

Word Wheels

- **WORD WHEELS** — 6, 7, 8, 9 & 10-letter word puzzles
- **WORD WHEELS** — 6-letter word puzzles
- **WORD WHEELS** — 7-letter word puzzles
- **WORD WHEELS** — 8-letter word puzzles

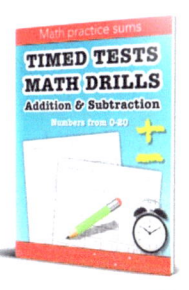

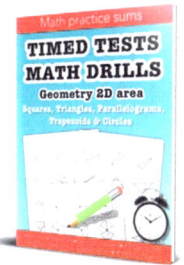

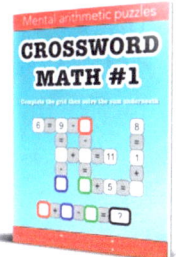

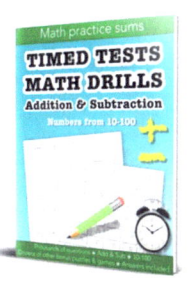

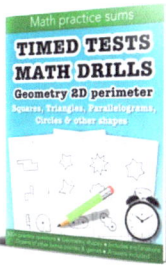

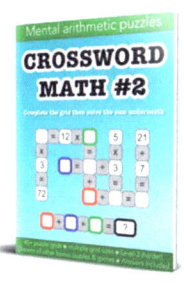

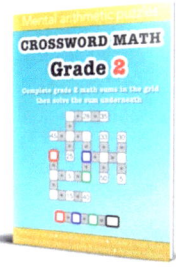

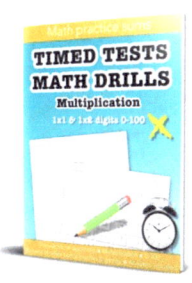

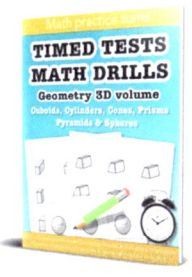

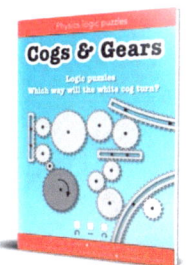

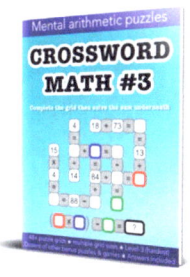

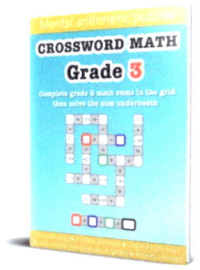

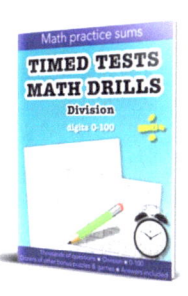

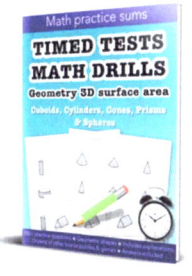

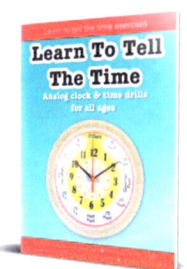

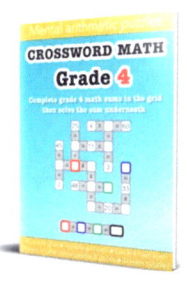

Math practice sums

Row 1 — Timed Tests Math Drills
- **Addition & Subtraction** — Numbers from 0-80
- **Addition & Subtraction** — Numbers from 10-100
- **Multiplication** — 1x1 & 1x2 digits 0-100
- **Division** — digits 0-100

Row 2 — Timed Tests Math Drills
- **Geometry 2D area** — Squares, Triangles, Parallelograms, Trapezoids & Circles
- **Geometry 2D perimeter** — Squares, Triangles, Parallelograms, Circles & other shapes
- **Geometry 3D volume** — Cuboids, Cylinders, Cones, Prisms, Pyramids & Spheres
- **Geometry 3D surface area** — Cuboids, Cylinders, Cones, Prisms & Spheres

Row 3
- **FRACTION CODES #1** — Match the letter to the fraction. Can you crack the codes?
- **TRAIN TRACKS LOGIC PUZZLES** — Lay the tracks from A to B. Test your logic and deduction skills
- **Cogs & Gears** — Physics logic puzzles. Which way will the white cog turn?
- **Balance Beam FORCES** — Mental arithmetic physics logic puzzles. Which way will the scales tip?

Row 4 — Mental arithmetic puzzles
- **CROSSWORD MATH #1** — Complete the grid then solve the sum underneath
- **CROSSWORD MATH #2** — Complete the grid then solve the sum underneath
- **CROSSWORD MATH #3** — Complete the grid then solve the sum underneath
- **Learn To Tell The Time** — Analog clock & time drills for all ages

Row 5 — Mental arithmetic
- **CROSSWORD MATH Grade 1**
- **CROSSWORD MATH Grade 2**
- **CROSSWORD MATH Grade 3**
- **CROSSWORD MATH Grade 4**

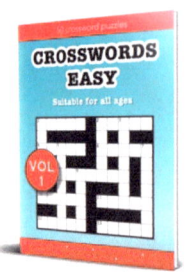

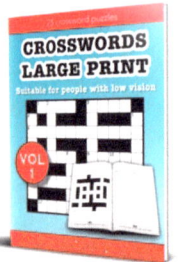

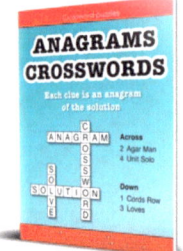

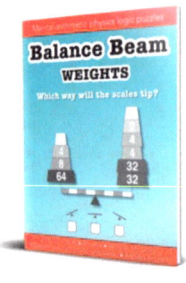

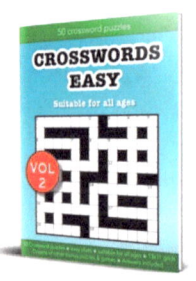

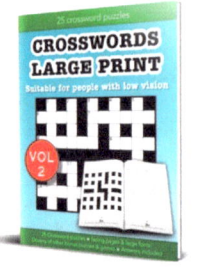

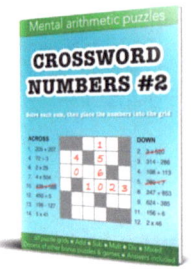

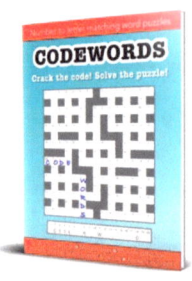

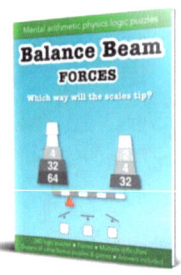

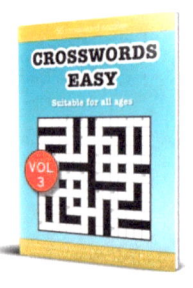

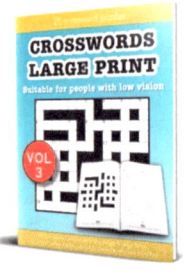

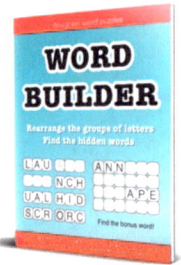

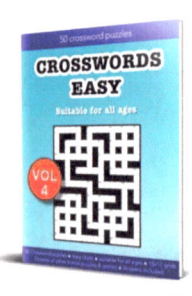

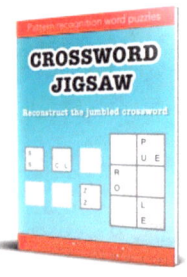

CROSSWORDS EASY Vol 1	CROSSWORDS EASY Vol 2	CROSSWORDS EASY Vol 3	CROSSWORDS EASY Vol 4
CROSSWORDS LARGE PRINT Vol 1	CROSSWORDS LARGE PRINT Vol 2	CROSSWORDS LARGE PRINT Vol 3	CROSSWORDS LARGE PRINT Vol 4
CROSSWORD NUMBERS #1	CROSSWORD NUMBERS #2	WORD BUILDER	WORD OVERLAP
ANAGRAMS CROSSWORDS	CODEWORDS	CROSSWORD ALPHABET	CROSSWORD JIGSAW
Balance Beam WEIGHTS	Balance Beam FORCES	WORD FILL-IN	MIXED ACTIVITY PUZZLES for adults

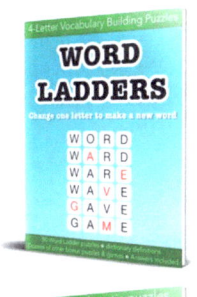

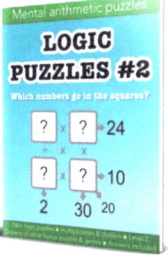

Puzzle Book Series

Word Ladders
- **Word Ladders** (3-Letter Vocabulary Building Puzzles) — Change one letter to make a new word 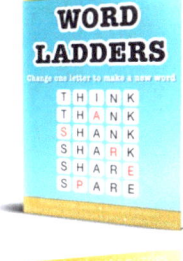
- **Word Ladders** (4-Letter Vocabulary Building Puzzles) — Change one letter to make a new word 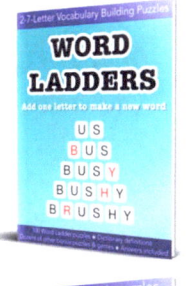
- **Word Ladders** (5-Letter Vocabulary Building Puzzles) — Change one letter to make a new word
- **Word Ladders** (2-7-Letter Vocabulary Building Puzzles) — Add one letter to make a new word

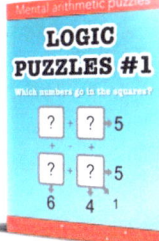

Logic Puzzles (Mental arithmetic puzzles)
- **Logic Puzzles #1** — Which numbers go in the squares?
- **Logic Puzzles #2** — Which numbers go in the squares? 
- **Logic Puzzles #3** — Which numbers go in the squares?
- **Logic Puzzles #4** — What is each picture worth?

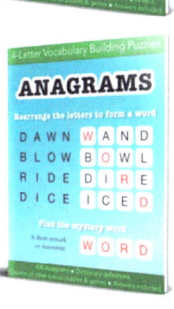

Anagrams
- **Anagrams** (3-Letter Vocabulary Building Puzzles) — Rearrange the letters to form a word 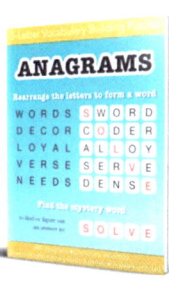
- **Anagrams** (4-Letter Vocabulary Building Puzzles) — Rearrange the letters to form a word
- **Anagrams** (5-Letter Vocabulary Building Puzzles) — Rearrange the letters to form a word 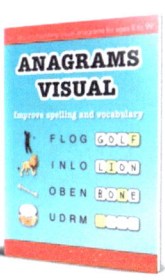
- **Anagrams Visual** — Improve spelling and vocabulary

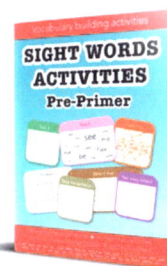

Sight Words Activities (Vocabulary building activities)
- **Sight Words Activities** — Pre-Primer
- **Sight Words Activities** — Primer
- **Sight Words Activities** — 1st Grade 
- **Sight Words Activities** — 2nd Grade
- **Sight Words Activities** — 3rd Grade

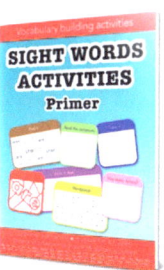

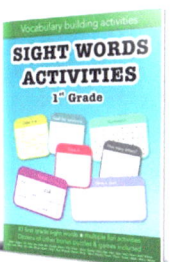

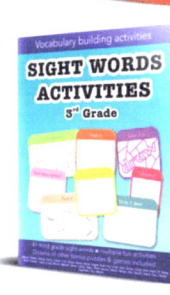

Make (Mental arithmetic puzzles)
- **Make 10** — Which numbers add up to 10 in a straight line?
- **Make 11** — Which numbers add up to 11 in a straight line?
- **Make 12** — Which numbers add up to 12 in a straight line?

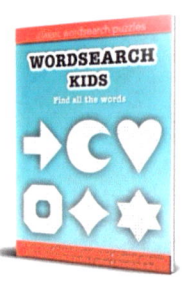

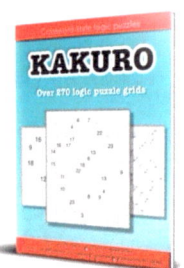

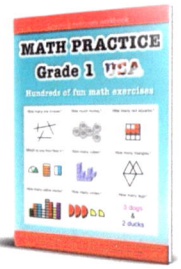

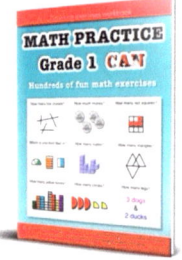

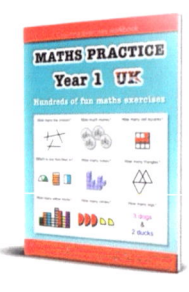

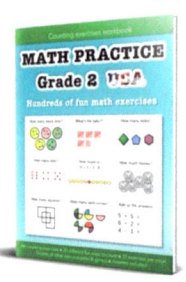

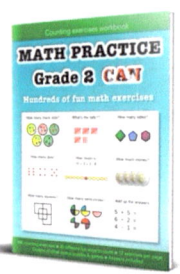

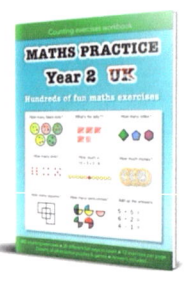

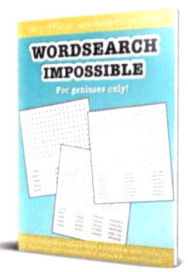

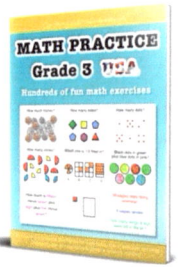

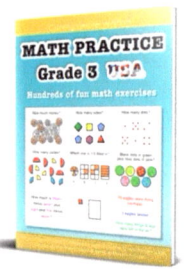

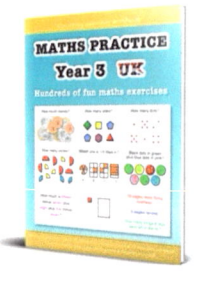

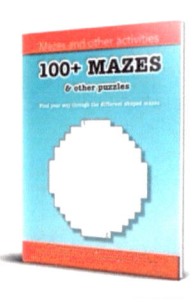

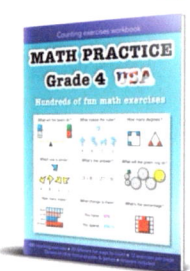

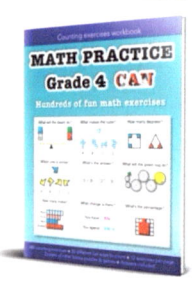

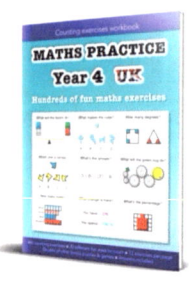

WORDSEARCH KIDS	**WORDSEARCH LARGE PRINT**	**WORDSEARCH IMPOSSIBLE**	**100+ MAZES**
KAKURO	**NUMBER SEARCH #1**	**HEX WORDS**	**WORD CROSS**
MATH PRACTICE Grade 1 USA	**MATH PRACTICE Grade 2 USA**	**MATH PRACTICE Grade 3 USA**	**MATH PRACTICE Grade 4 USA**
MATH PRACTICE Grade 1 CAN	**MATH PRACTICE Grade 2 CAN**	**MATH PRACTICE Grade 3 USA**	**MATH PRACTICE Grade 4 CAN**
MATHS PRACTICE Year 1 UK	**MATHS PRACTICE Year 2 UK**	**MATHS PRACTICE Year 3 UK**	**MATHS PRACTICE Year 4 UK**

Made in the USA
Columbia, SC
08 May 2024